MW01141255

RESTORATION

A Time of Renewal

by
Elder James M. Martin

J. M. Martin Publishing
P.O. Box 27364
Lansing, MI 48909

Printed in the United States of America
Morris Publishing
3212 East Highway 30
Kearney, NE 68847
1-800-650-7888

To Cora, my wife, and children

To my mother, Mertria who lay the foundation for my minstry.

And many wonderful friends across the country for your prayers and support

FOREWORD

It is awe-inspiring to see the power of restoration at work, whether it is in the nature of events, the change in people's lives, or in spiritual transformation. Its effects bewilder us, and yet history testifies that all of us become devastated without its aid.

Starting in Chapter One, we will take a mental journey into the history of "restoration," and its meaning in the adjective form; we will proceed to look at its divertive operation throughout the ages. The story of restoration in this book will then progressively move toward the nation of Israel, cataloguing the important but complex struggles for restoration that it has experienced.

The objective of this book is to provide the reader with a reliable, comprehensive guidance for spiritual restoration, and as well as teaching its applicability in both in the natural and biblical developments. Hopefully, while revitalizing is taking place with you, you'll be encouraged to continue to rebuild other lives as well.

Restoration

A Time of Renewal

He refreshes and restores my life; He leads me in the paths of righteousness for his name sake. Psalms 23:3

Contents

I AM A WINNER!

IN TRIBULATIONS AND PAIN
DOES GOD'S SUSTAIN
HE CAN PULL SWEET OUT OF BITTERNESS
With POWER, AND MIGHT, WHEN WE PRAY.

SO, I SAY TO MYSELF, MARCH ON MY BELOVED,
CONQUER WHAT YOU CAN THIS DAY.
IF BY TRYING YOU SHOULD NOT SUCCEED,
KEEP A WINNERS ATTITUDE, AND
PRAISE THE NAME OF THE LORD ANYWAY.

TAKE DESPAIR BY ITS BULL'S HORN AND
CAST IT DOWN BY FAITH.
WHO CAN SAY, I NOT A WINNER NOW?
SEEING, I HAVE WON THIS BATTLE TODAY!

by James M. Martin

PART I

Imperative Reasons
for
Restoration

Chapter 1

What is Restoration

Throughout the ages restoration has faithfully carried the earth's burdens on its shoulders while supplying it with its liveliness; an fulfillment that has been as extraordinary as the orbiting planets that surround us and yet be as comely as a man. In an adjective sense of speaking, restoration is considered as old as time itself. When the world was first made, restoration was present during the process. When God said in the (Genesis 1:1-23), "Let there be . . ." 'Restoration took a step forward and bowed before the Almighty God and suddenly, a world that was void and without form became a world of magnificent nature; pure and full of glory.

So as the world with its inhabitants turn with its daily business, so must the power of restoration turn with it; if it didn't, the world would be most miserable.

11

To appreciate restoration is to appreciate the brilliant essence of what life should be. While we do benefit from its power, no one can measure the height or depth of its goodness, or accurately determine its width. Who can track its course and describe the multiple functions of its operations? History has faithfully declared that when the hand of the benevolent transforms a place or person, nature will bring forth its praise. Hearts will leap for joy and voices will gladly sing.

The power and effects of restoration are like the trembling leaves on a Sugar Maple tree. At a glance it is one of the most magnificent displays in the entire plant kingdom. The autumnal "over all other trees," describes Donald Peattie, a author, "will stand tall with its clearest yellow, richest crimson, tumultuous scarlet, or brilliant orange - the yellow pigments shining through the over-painting of the red foliage of Sugar Maple will at once outdo and yet, unify the rest of nature." It is like the mighty, marching melody that rides upon the crest of some symphonic weltering sea and, with its crying song, give meaning to all the calculated dissonance of the orchestra."[1]

Like Peattie way of describing the tree most people sometime will attempt to give their description of restoration on their lives in the same grand fashion as well, but in different perspectives. One may describe restoration and its effects like a tree - old, strong, and standing tall; others will accentuate its statuesque quality in a song or joyful praise. Others will cry and tremble because of the wonderful feelings and effects, and through the wonderful experiences will appeal to the love of joy it brings. Still others will attempt to extract the complete structure of revivification in their lives with intricacy of detail. [2]

While returning back to Portland, Oregon from a preaching engagement in Kent, Washington, I decide to ask my sister, Mertria, who was with me as to how she felt being restored back to God. Mertria apply that she felt good and start rocking her body from side to side with light gestures with her hands. She hums a tune typical type of sounds with persons that were very happy to be release from something treble in their past. Suddenly, she begin engaging in very loud praises to God, her arms shot straight up in the air; screamed to the top of her voice-"Hu'le-le-lu'jah,Thank you, Jesus." Mertria did this sporadically. Of course, I understood what was taken place with her, however, each time she would scream and shake, the car seem to rock with her body and I was getting little worry that we had not gone too far from Seattle, Washington on Interstate 5, the traffic was getting heavy and we still had less than one hundred miles to go before getting home.

An little nervous, I ask her if she was fine. She applies, "James, I just don't know, I can't explain it... All I know is, I feel like tons of weight have been lifted off of me." Smiling, I knew and was happy about what she was talking about. My sister had been wonderfully delivered from the bondage of sin just over a year ago, and she still couldn't come with the right words to describe to people the type of restoration that Jesus Christ, the Son of God, had wrought in her life.

The problem is, even with the best of description that Peattie and my sister try to give of restoration, it is still complex in its operations and effects, and its function is ever-changing. However, when a situation in our lives has been changed into good by the force of restoration, all of us together will come away seeing the grace, dignity, or strength of the power revivification had. The power of restoration is awesome, like that of the particular tree mention earlier. The fact that restoration with its pomp and glory will still connote different meanings to different people is a fact none can deny.

Restoration in the basic sense, actually means something that is restored, especially a representation or reconstruction of the original form with some components of restoration being used in a diversity of circumstances or belongings, such as repainting an old family car or house, putting new finish on a antique furniture, restoring of bad credit, or even renewing bad relationships among friends or family. Nevertheless, lets deal with the historical end of those powerful, but various words of restoration and see what history has to say about it.

Restoration as a common word may have made its imprint into history as early as the 14th century. Note some of the key words below that were used to provide change for the better.

Reinstatement

Refurbishment

Reestablishment

Return

Restitution

Reinstallation

In many cases, evidence of the utilization of these words such as reinstatement, refurbishment, or even reestablishments, can be found intertwined into the very fabric of objects, people, and even old buildings.

However, there are several types of restorations that I would like to discuss that served as an adjective to this old English term during its frequent use in the 17th and 18th century but may not have filtered into the common terms of use in modern English. The terms are interesting and are good reasons to reflect upon those who with deep thanks can appreciate different aspects of restoration and its power on people's lives.

Res'toress

This term, res'toress, refer to a female restorer. Pusey, Edward Bouverie (1800-82), was a British clergyman and theologian, a leader of the Oxford movement, believes that Mary, the mother of Jesus was rightly called Redemptress, Restoress . . . and the cause of our Salvation.[3] To put it more clearly, Mary was indeed the perfect channel through which God, in his infinite wisdom chose to bring through forth the Redeemer and Savior of the World. To apply that term to Mary as the mother of Jesus Christ is good; however, the generally attributes associated with that word seem to fit other great women of the bible and contemporary history.

Deborah, a prophetess, the wife of Lappidoth, was leading Israel at that time. [4] She held court under the Palm of Deborah between Ramah and Bethel in the hill country of Ephraim, and the Israelites came to her to have their disputes decided. Judges 4:4-5 (NIV)

Deborah was apparently an effective judge and leader of her people in Israel. It was the leader's responsibly to sit at the gate or some designated place and settle disputes between parties. I suppose it would be no different today. A problem is a problem regardless of its nature. She was also a warrior, and though married to Lappidoth, she helped Barak defeat the Sisera army (Judges 4:6-16). Could this woman of God fit the description of a restoree?

And what about Esther, the Queen as mentioned in the Book of Esther. Esther saved king Ahasuerus life from a plot against him by two of his chamberlains, Bigthan and Teresh who usually kept the door at the palaces in (Esther 2:21-23). Esther also interceded for Mordecai, her uncle, and the Jewish people from Haman's plotted to destroy them, (Esther 3:1-15)! Nevertheless, the strategy and risk that this beautiful, graceful queen undertaken to block Haman's schemes to get the King's permission to destroy her people in Book of Esther, (Chapter 5 and 6), is remarkable indeed. Surly, she could qualify to be a restoree, or the instrument of deliverances for her people, I think?

In 1932, Dr. Matilda Moldenhauer Brooks, a research associate in biology at the University of California, found two effective antidotes to two of the quickest and most deadly poisons. If she had not found the cure, would there be an alarming death rate for victims from cyanide and carbon monoxide poisoning? [5]

Clara Barton, a former schoolteacher and patent clerk volunteer to go to the front line to serve in the Civil War. While there, she instrumental in saving thousands of soldiers lives during the Civil War in 1861. And she also serves in Paris during the 1871 revolution. [5] Could this woman of God fit the description of a restoree?

The list could go on and on. I counted over 300 women in just one women's history book that have labored to relieve others from suffering. But we must settle here for now that the role-play of a restoree as far as its historical term is concerned can be extended and expanded to refer to any woman, past, present or future who willingly makes herself available to God. History books testify loud and clear to that.

Restoratonist

"Dean B. B Edwards's Encyclopedia" defines Restoratonist as The Independent Messenger . . . devoted to the cause of Restoratonism. Also, the restoratonist mean one who restores old dilapidated buildings, that term is dealt with in more detail in Chapter Two. The term, restoratonism is a doctrinal belief that came into use sometime around 1800's which taught that all men are ultimately restored to a state of happiness in the future life. [6] The doctrine was correct in part, with the

17

exception of two key words - "all men." The bible does not support that belief of "all men." Rather, those who are born-again believers in Christ, will be restored to a state of happiness in the future life. Examples of this can be found in (Matthew 5:12), which says none but the pure in heart shall see God. Other scriptures offer proof: (Revelation 21:7,8); (Matt 5:1-12); (1Peter 4:17,18). These are a fraction of scriptures that clearly state who will witness a state of happiness in the end.

Hank Hanegraaff, an author, stated that Charles Parham, as one of the global revivalists, uses the term restoratonism as to include or to fully mean end-time restoratonism. Charles Parham believes that at the end of the age God will restore supernatural signs, "super apostles, and prophets." He goes on to state that he, along with other end-time preachers, believes that no prophet or apostle who ever lived will equal the power of these individuals in the great army of the Lord - not even Elijah or Peter or Paul.[7] Charles may be correct if he is referring to the numbers of souls be won to Christ over the last few decades; by all means we have far exceeded Paul, Elijah and Peter in reaching the people through the uses of television, radio, and now, the internet. We have had far better and faster transportation systems to take the gospel around the world. And millions have been won to Christ by these transportation and media means that are available. Many have been heal of numerals of conditions; I have seen great miracles taken place personally; there is no questions about that.

By all means, we should have had the opportunity

to do greater works as Jesus did say we would. (John 14:22). However, the claim that Charles makes about *end-time preachers* would *supercede* the level of miracles <u>*we read about*</u> in the bible that Elijah, Peter or Paul performed is something I haven't seen yet, and it is consider debatable by social critics and believers alike. I believe each person through out the church world must individually judge that statement of Charles Parham for themselves; thus, for the sake of the record, it is better to stick with the point to how the word, <u>*restoratonism,*</u> was claim to be use by Charles here, rather than be controvertible with the *level* and *kinds* of miracles that has actually took place over the last few decades.

Restorative

In Uncle Tom's Cabin there is a story about St. Claire suffering through a fainting spell; however, as Miss Ophelia applied restoratives, he revived and opened his eyes. Fortunately, there were restoratives available.

No one can experience restoration in his or her life unless there is an instrument available to supply it. In the case of St. Claire, the medications that were apply serve as the effective instrument through which renewal of his health came. In the general sense, it doesn't matter how the person, or a thing is affected, the instrument that is responsible for the work of restoration lies with the supplier.

Spiritual side of restoration
Restorer

However, the awesome dynamism of restoration we see taken place in the natural realm of life around us will also have it effect in similitude or even greater to the spiritual part of our lives as well, except the work of that spiritual revivification or rehabilitation in one's life is done primarily under the guidance of God's power through people he chooses to use. The bible teaches that it is through God's benevolent acts alone that we can receive substantial redemption from bad habits, broken spirits, and bad past, etc.

Restoration, which was used commonly in the 1400s and 1600s, may have gotten its name from the Hebrew word "hadas," meaning to restore, restored, (to renew or repair). In the New Testament, several Greek words are translated restore. Acts 15:16 speaks of restoration of Davidic rule, and uses anorthoo meaning set up, erects again. [8]

In the Book of Isaiah, the word restored is graciously used concerning Israel coming back to their promised land. Isaiah 10:22.

David uses the word to express being refreshed by God, in (Psalm 23:3). In the development of the messianic concept, however, the meaning of the term was narrowed down to the redeemer and restorer of the Jewish nation.

(2) The kings of the earth take their stand and the rulers gather together against the LORD and against his Anointed One. Psalms 2:2 (NIV)

In (Psalms 85:6), David asks God to revive us (Israel) again that the people may rejoice in thee. Again in another case:

And the vessel that he was making of clay was spoiled in the hand of the potter, so he made it over, reworking it into another vessel, as it seemed good to the potter to make it. Then the word of the Lord came to me. O house of Israel, cannot I do with you as this potter? Says the Lord. Behold, as the clay is in the potter's hand, so are you in my hand, O house of Israel. But if the people of that nation, concerning which I have spoken, turn from their evil, I will relent and reverse My decision concerning the evil that I thought to do to them. Jeremiah 18:1-6,8

In this powerful passage, the prophet Jeremiah paints a picture of Israel being in the Potter's (God) hand. However, the clay (Israel) strangely became marred, that is, messed up. Nevertheless, the Potter (God) loved the clay so much that he was willing to work out a redemption process where Israel could repent and be restored back to its former glory, something only the Divine Potter could do.

(13) Then he said to the man, "Stretch out your hand." So he stretched it out and it was completely restored, just as sound as the other. Matt 12:13 (NIV)

(25) Once more Jesus put his hands on the man's eyes. Then his eyes were opened, his sight was restored, and he saw everything clearly. Mark 8:25 (NIV)

(18) Who had come to hear him and to be healed of their diseases? Those troubled by evil spirits were cured. (19) And the people all tried to touch him, because power was coming from him

and healing them all. Luke 6:18-19 (NIV)

Jesus Christ, as the Son of God, was then, and still is a master philanthropist; for he brought complete restoration to many of his followers, as indicated in the in Matthew, Mark, Luke and John, disciples, who follow Jesus closely, and also wrote copiously of his restorative-type ministry. And, in all cases, whether a person had a withered hand, blind eyes, or an incurable disease, they went away with the opportunity to live normal lives again. According to (Luke 19:10); and (John 10:10), Jesus says explicitly in scripture, that his mission on earth was to save people that were lost - also, that those who lack life, he would give them life and that more abundantly.

If that was Christ's makeup, then, should that be Christ's followers' makeup and objective as well? And for Christians to avoid doing the very mission that Christ have already done and also has commanded us to do means to deny restoration.

Chapter 2

The Search for Restoration

In all our lives there is the need for some fulfillment whether the fulfillment comes from some personal item, a new physical look, securing some emotional ties, or simply completing a desired project, people crave the subsequent emotion. The desperation to fill that void often leaves painful longing in the heart and leads people to vigilantly search for clues or answers. There is no escape from this pain of reality. To further explain this, vigilantly, or crave' search for restoration, I will show the varied aspects of it with "things" or people, who search for restoration in the natural as well as the spiritual sense.

Restoration in the Sanctuary

Today, Notre Dame Cathedral stands as a model of calm and majesty, and is a serene emblem of its civilization. All its architectural components are easily recognizable: the three great sculptured portals, the

Gallery of Kings, the perfect rose window, and lovely open colonnade that stands tall above. The architectural glory of the Cathedral seems to move, breathe, and aspire to Heavenly heights. Notre Dame was built by a superb common effort in which the entire community took part. The Cathedral was a spectacular structure within the walled city of the Middle Ages. It is the organic heart of Paris, and from it flowed hope, confidence, joy, and exaltation.

The cathedral architecture design could, and did, serve as a home for all other arts, and reflect accurately, as nothing else could, the aesthetic climate of a nation. The Cathedral is the key to the health of a society. It is said that every road in France centers inwardly on the Cathedral. The Notre Dame structure has resisted all - fire, German bombs, Nazi raids - and yet it stood unconquerable and silent, mirroring the soul of its city. [1]

While traveling to Memphis, Tennessee, I visit Bountiful Blessings new sanctuary located on G. E. Patterson St. led by its leader, Bishop G.E. Patterson. This church, I notice quickly, has its own unique and beautiful design throughout its property; marvelous landscapes, big water fountain in the front part of the chruch; spacious lobby areas, business offices, classroom, bathrooms; a marvously reflective of the Mirage Hotel in Las Vegas Nevada. And, of course, the splendorous sanctuary, an architecture wonder that will inspire one with *'picturesque'* imagines of the Notre Dame Cathedral, if not closer to it; yet, Bountiful Blessing layout seem to reflect the soul of a conquering designer.

There are of course, many other such beautiful churches across the country that can boast of beauty as well, and, many of us come away feeling a sense of spiritual pride and joy about that church and its ministries as well. And, with some reflection, look at King David, who too, in the Old Testament, desired to build God a house (church). This temple were to be exceeding *magnificence*, of *fame,* and *glory* throughout the world. (1 Chronicles 22:5). And, apart from its architecture glory, we pray and hope that same beautiful temple we visit would always be fill with the glory of God, being an outlet for others as it was to us through which the wounded, the helpless, and the broken hearten person could find restoration.

> *The house of God was filled with a cloud, so that the priests could not stand to minister by reason of the cloud, for the glory of the Lord had filled the house of God. 2 Chronicles 5:13,14.*

And regardless where that church was, it brings to all of us each time we visit, a restorative message of hope, confidence, joy and exaltation; somewhere within that temple we visited was a spot where "all" could find solace with God in prayer and worship. (Psalm 27:4). We go away with relief in our spirits, perhaps huming a tune while leaving, happy that we have found restoration again, in that *beautiful house* of God.

Search for Self-esteem

In 1890 the Stanton-Anthony group merged with

the Stone-Beecher faction to form the National American Woman Suffrage Association. The organization's many arguments pointed to centuries of social, political and cultural abuse against women. Among women's concerns were obtaining representation in government matters, equal pay in the workplace, the right to serve on juries, the right to retain earnings and property after marriage, and protection against disgraceful behavior against women. Most importantly, they wanted the right to vote.

Apart from their homes, women obviously felt they were being cruelly dominated by a world that seemed to belong to men, and with no opportunity to show their competence to fill social roles held by only men. The Suffrage Association worked to advance women's rights on both the state and federal levels. The American suffragist movement scored its climactic victory shortly after World War I. In 1919 Congress approved the 19th Amendment to the U.S. Constitution, which provided that "The right of citizens of the United States to vote shall not be denied or abridged by the United States or by any State on account of sex." Ratified on August 18, 1920, the 19th Amendment became the law of the land. [2]

Freedom from Bondage

It was not until the Emancipation of Independence from Slavery Act was signed into law in 1865 that blacks could dream of the day that annihilation of slavery that had destroy their self-worth or existence as a race of people would one day be eliminated forever into the past.

Black people during slavery endured widespread exploitation, paternalism, and brutal abuse – even the whipping of very small children. Black mothers were used as human breeders and their babies would be forcibly wrenched from their arms and sold to a different slave owner. Blacks had no say and no rights and were considered of less value than cattle. This would be a clear-cut case of the obliteration of a person's importance to society. Susan Banfield, an author, writes, "in addition to physical punishment, an elaborate set of regulations, known as "slave codes," were enacted to keep slaves ignorant and under the thumb of their white masters. [3]

Freedom fighters Nat Turner, Gabriel Prosser, Denmark Vesey, and many other white and black abolitionists who obviously studied the Declaration of Independence quickly used the language of the document, which says in part, "all men were created equal," as a successful challenge against slavery in the Antebellum South. The continual cry for the black race's liberation eventually led Northern states to free slaves within their borders in the 1780s, 1790s and early 1800s, with final success of abolition of slavery by Abraham Lincoln, sixteenth President of the United States of America in 1865. [4]

Looking for the right answers
Restoration movements among religious bodies are not new and involve many. According to Richard T. Hughes in The American Quest for the Primitive Church, there have been strong restoration sentiments in American Judaism, American Catholicism, and in other

religious movements in the United States. As early as 1729, the Puritans, the Anglican Evangelical had restoratonist ideologies. The Church of Jesus Christ of Latter-day Saints started its restoration movement in 1820, the Church of Christ in 1809, Church of God and Church of God in Christ in the 1900's. These restoration movements would include Baptists, Methodists, Episcopalians, and other fundamentalists. [5]

Rev. Stanley E. Jones, in his entitled book," *The Reconstruction of the Church.*" quoted this statement from a social critic's source:

"The center of criticism from social critics of the world is this: the church is irrelevant. It is not related to the problems of the day. It is guarding values that are no longer valuable. It is not geared into the problems and issues of modern life.   I once stood on a hill in Central India. On the top of that hill was a fort, guarded by soldiers in their long uniforms and holding pikes. Once the center of that feudal state that fort was relevant, it held the authority and power of the state within its four thick walls. But the center of power and authority had moved beyond those thick walls; it had moved up the valley with the center of the city now. The fort, now high and dry - and irrelevant; no longer needed. But soldiers were still pompously guarding that "*irrelevance fort.*" [6]

Rev. Jones who noted this statement from the critic's strongly disagrees as most of us would but admit there are weak areas that needs attention. History does reveal that there exist within the soul of humanity a quest for restoration which drives a person to ascertain the relevance of religion movement's traditional values or teachings in order to feel secure. Could the example of this *irrelevant fort* be possibly one of the many important reasons why people begin new restoration movements? If that particular movement or church fails to provide clear answers or show substantive prove that its doctrinal teaching is sound enough, the searcher of restoration will become disenchanted and declare the movement's doctrinal position "irrelevance," that is, the church is pompously guarding principals and values no longer effective for the current times. He or she would thus feel compelled to seek for change or join another church, or may even develop his or her own movement; thus, new values and ideas for restoration are given birth-an new movement. Most of us have seen this happen plenty of times.

For example: Thomas Campbell, a Seceder Presbyterian minister, felt at odds with his church over the authority of Scripture as compared with creeds and the limitations of fellowship at the Lord's Table. When matters could not be resolved he felt led to withdraw his fellowship from the Presbyterian Church and in 1809 began the Church of Christ restoration movement. [7]

While leaders like Campbell, Bishop Charles H. Mason and others great leaders have gone on to build tremendous ministries, even out of its own organizations have other movements been developed since. In fact, there are over three hundred different faiths in United States of America alone, and most of them were born out of some religious movement that was already well-established! The question of whether such movements as the Church of Christ, Methodist, or any other religious movement mentioned here in this chapter is biblical sound or correct in its foundational concepts is not the focus here; God Almighy alone has that sovereign right to judge such movements and he will ultimately decare the rightness or wrong of "all" such movements at the end of the church age. In fact the most important focus point here is, to shed light on religions Movements' search for revivification and opportunity to expand its message of renewal through development and common fellowship which sufficiently explains the writer's position with people's overall search for restoration. The search for regeneration of a soul will continue everywhere and with many more people starting new ministries! History does distinctly teach that the soul of man confronted by bitterness, pain, and discontent will long desperately for some type of spiritual insight. Unless someone comes forth to provide the perfect answers to such concerns, the wheels of religious movements that have been struggling to turn the ruin in our lives into new beginnings will never need to turn again. Those fighting to supply spiritual restoration will continue to roll so long as the need for restoration of humanity stands.

Obsession for a New Look

In 1998, plastic surgeons performed an estimated 2.1 million cosmetic procedures such as nose lifts, lipovaccine, body trimming, and collagen injections for people frantic for a new look. Since 1992 there has been a 50% increase in these cosmetic procedures making the quest for a new look somewhat of an obsession with 40% or more people. The trend is still growing at an alarming rate and has become a grave concern among some medical observers. Restoration of the body is no doubt a serious matter, but also means big profit for those who are able to supply the demand.

Finding my Self-Worth

Ask any man who contemplates the prospect of spending his life suffering from the stigma of a short stature, slurred speech, and impoverished status whether he would exchange that fate for being tall, speaking melodiously, and having plenty of money, and the answer would obviously be a ringing affirmation.

Though I became a born-again Christian in 1973 and entered the ministry shortly thereafter, I still suffer from low self-esteem episodes that stem from categorization by others during my formative years. To have endured this as a child and now to face the same fate as adult - I would gladly exchange shoes with someone without a moment's hesitation.

This obviously became a problem in 1973 while working at St. Mary's Hospital in Reno, Nevada and also serving as a youth pastor at one of the local Pentecostal churches. I remember when I would, at times, spend my entire energy trying to win acceptance from certain people, especially those of my age and yes, there was still that hunger to be what I was not. Tragically, I stood alone, and was most afraid that if I tried again, that unwritten message - " you are not on our level" - would appear on people's faces, and I would be tempted to erupt in anger. At that point I felt trapped, fearful, and apprehensive. "Was this the way Christian life was supposed to be?" The more I thought about it the more the anticipation of disaster seemed to increase. I began looking at myself, and also the situations around with me with a mix of loathing and fear. No one ever knew the depth of my misery.

For several weeks while deliberated over what direction to go I managed to save up over a thousand dollars by working two jobs. I was desperately in need of a car and while looking in the car ads, I noticed a big car sale in Sacramento, California and decided to attend. Upon arrival, I began looking around for cars that were in the thousand dollar range. A salesman came out and greeted me and notice me looking at a dark brown Pontiac, 69 model GTO, with wide sport wheels, cream color buckle seats, stereo tape deck - the whole works. This car was the sharpest vehicle I had ever seen! The salesman told me that the car could be finance on credit which was something new to me? He then took me into the office to fill out the papers, and later told me to wait while he went to talk to the credit manager about my credit application. A big knot was begining to tighten in my stomach, nervous, I sat and waited; my head driping with sweat.

Several minutes later the man came back smiling and said that the loan had been approved. I believe I had a stunned look on my face, but then, filled with emotion, I started to jump up do a victory dance, Indian or American style, but decided to hold my peace and reluctantly handed him the thousand dollars for the down payment. Was I dreaming this, or was he kidding me? Could this be true? My ability to respond to the finance officer'altered. Smiling, the guys looked at me and assured me I didn't need to worry. It was not until I was well on my way toward home that it actually hit me; you have just brought a car. Your first car! Immediately, the cap that had laid center on my head was pulled to one side as I slid lower into the car seat singing one of my victory songs. For once in my life, everything was changing for good!

Back into Reno I decide to go to some clothing stores in search for more newer, expensive brand clothes, mostly in brown shades colors to blend in with the brown color tone of the car. Though small in frame I insisted that the clothing shop would need to find a way for the clothes to fit on me right. I wasn't accepting no for an answer too easily. Every part of my defeated emotion took a 190-degree turnabout and from that point began to feel better about myself. In fact, I was so proud of the car and myself that I would go from one church member's house to another to show off the car. And, to add more fuel to my already reinvigorated personality, the pastor compliments me and said he thought the car was sharp and becoming. Boy, that put the cap on everything. Even my attitude about people's negative behavior toward me in the past was slowly beginning to change; and if they were saying something negative, it didn't matter; an important part of my self-worth was now restored.

Yes, those experiences happened over twenty-five years ago; I was only twenty-one years old, spiritually immature, and new into the ministry. But, out of this emotional womb was born a new man destined one day to train and inspire others as to how they could rebuild their own motivation and self-esteem. And it all started with a 1969 G.T.O. Pontiac.

Chapter 3

Life Without Restoration

For whatever were thus written in the former days was written for our instruction, or whatever were thus written in, that by our steadfast, and patient may endurance the test to **draw** from the Scriptures tightly our hope. **Roman** 15:4 These things happened to them as examples and were written down as warning for us, on whom the fulfillment of the ages has come. Be careful! (1 Corinthians 10:11)

According to Apostle Paul, all the past event(s) that was written in the bible has already establish for us essential information and vital examples in its scriptures for each believer; but if you would note the two scriptures side by side, they are given in contrast languages. While (Roman 15:4) scriptures provide vital examples where a person could systemically glean and develop a working knowledge to be successful in God;

the other scripture, (l Corinthians 10:11), details another type of example(s) and information: read (l Corinthian 10:1-10). Paul clearly details Israel's unfavorable behavior toward God in the Old Testament and points out the punishment that they received for not following God's laws; its all there. In other words, after we get finish reading the Old and New Testament examples, good and bad, which one should we follow next? To that question, each must individually answer.

One thing is certain, our actions will eventually prove or manifest an incorporating level of understanding of the scriptures, or it will prove that we did not learn from the scripture, hence, it will show our failures. At the same time, we can also trace the same kind of pattern with success or failures to events recorded in natural history as well.

Elvis Presley was one of the most honored and adored singers in history, and sold an estimated one billion records during his singing career. Better known as the King of Rock and Roll, he amassed every material and worldly prize one could attain, but it could not provide *meaning* and *significance* for his aching human heart. He was like a little boy seeking love and affection, and the adoration of his fans was like a *"fix'* to a junkie. Whenever it was denied him, he suffered from bouts of depression and self-doubt – he longed to be loved. Friends of our family that knew Elvis say he grew up in an Assembly of God church in Tupelo, Mississippi.

His last ten years of life were consumed by his

addiction to illegal substances and alcohol. With this abusive life-styles, and misconceptions with various religions, he wandered down the road of despair, depression, and confusion. He finally died on August 16, 1977. [1]

Elvis Presley's penchant for quick fixes, his selfish behavior, and his other predacious means to get by failed him. Elvis's wealth could not *surfeit*, or *subtract* the above-mentioned ruin in his life, nor could it subvert the hollowness. Despite his ample wealth, Elvis needed *restoration in his life* of which none of his wealth could help him attain.

The writer mentioned earlier about Elvis Presley; let's now move into history again.

As a child, Adolf Hitler was always considered a problem, even in school. He was unpopular, lazy, uncooperative, and a troublemaker who consistently lied and was very secretive states Walter C. Langer, writer and retired private psychoanalytic. Werner Maser, writer, and director of the Institute for Studies in Contemporary History in Husum said in his book that people who have claimed to know him only 'knew' what Hitler would deliberately let 'slip' out. Later in his political career he developed and perfected the art of manipulation while stirring crowds into a fury in support of his political platforms, and yet, he was as Mr. Maser describes, distant, withdrawn, critical, and impatient, especially to those he disliked. Indeed, he was a strange and a troubled man.

Adolph Hitler nearly succeeded in his dream of gaining control of the world. He was like a person with a passion for something within easy reach and he went after it. Mr. Ray Wright, an author, says that Hitler's deceptive personality went unnoticed, the masses played right into his rule, and they allowed him to systematically undermine the Weimer Constitution by exploiting the very freedom it granted him. He engineered The Enables Act, which created laws he designed solely to use terror tactics against any people who opposed him ... primarily Jewish people. Six million Jews died as a result of Hitler's political position.

It appears from all history reports that Hitler exceeded in stockpiling enough power, money, and political prestige, including an incredible human arsenal, to carry out his mission. Yet, during his last few months in office were days he feared abandonment and misery. He never learned that his resources couldn't give peace or happiness.

Mr. Langer says that Hitler had fears of being poisoned, being assassinated, fears of losing his health, fears of gaining weight, fear of treason, and fears of losing his mystical guidance, or facing death and for that reason he could not sleep. [2] The friends that he had in his life could not fill the empty, loathsome spot in his heart. History books characterize Hitler as a monster out of touch with reality, selfish, lacking sound judgment, distrusts everyone, even those closest to him. Though he needs love, he could not establish any close friendship without the pain or fear of being betrayed. [3]

Adolf Hitler needed a spiritual transformation of which only God, as the loving Father, could only do for him. According to H.R. Trevor-Roper in his book entitled, "The Last Days of Hitler," say that Adolf Hitler planned his own suicide in his private bunker by shooting himself through the mouth while his wife swallowed poison. Both were found dead at 3:30p.m.

What are the trouble signs?

1. Demoniac like personalities.
2. Ministries intercepted by satan.
3. Financial bondages.
4. Generation family bloodline curses.
5. Deteriorate feelings, spiritual or naturally.
6. Spiritual and physical addictions, "fixes".

The above list may only serve as a partial listing of broken restoration and you are welcome to reflect on this list and add to this calamitous pile. When you finish, we must agree that the sum of the whole will still equal to a *"lack of restoration."*

The fact that lack of restoration only fits those not involved in church is remised. Let's move closer to home where these cases of "lack of restoration" was found interweave into my own mother's life who suffered from a family bloodline curses which were passed down to her from her own generation. Mother Martin, as she was know in Portland, Oregon, had no idea about generation curses even when she died in 1998 at the age of 81 years old from multiple illness. She knew she had been rob by satan, but could not figure out the reasons why? Though Mother Martin was a deeply committed saint, however, the children believes she could have lived a longer and an happier life if aware what was going on in time in her life. Mother marry at a very young age, and soon began experiencing failed marriages. The reasons surrounding the fail marriages was puzzlingly and strange to the family. It is widely believed that satan was frighten of the spiritual gifts that God had deposited into mother's life and sought to perpetrate her ruin with the generation family curse. Along with struggles to raise a large family alone, Mother Martin receive harsh criticisms from people that made her cry often and be very upset; including a demoniac guilt and deteriorate feelings from satan which only compounded problems for her more worse.

In reflection, we know that these problems with the family bloodline curse that satan shrewdly impose upon my mother were nothing more than a spiritual attack to destroy the awesome grace she had with God in her life and to block the well-being of her own progeny.

Unfortunately, her children also inherited some of the traits of her problems, even into our adulthood. Like a sheep led to the slaughter, we too, innocently, was targeted by satan. Needless to say, my mother earnestly prayed for *restorative type* blessings upon her family and wanted to see it come to past in her lifetime. All of us are now thankful though, that in sprite of the things Mother Martin went through in her life she was herself spiritually restored long before she past away to be with the Lord, but the *restorative type* blessings she labored in prayer for her children and wanted to see happen before she passed away did not take place until shortly after her death.

Those *restorational* blessings," however, was conditional with each family member.   First, we must think twice before entering any kind of venture, such as marriage, financial opportunities, society involvement, etc. Also, if mistakes were made, admit it, and be willing to pay the price for recovery. At the same time, be persistent against the demoniacal attacks through prayer and spiritual discipline.

Here is another case:

Years ago, a young lady, we will call her Jean, attended one of the local Pentecost churches in Arkansas would confide in me about her problems, and of course, she appeared to be emotional depressed. If things weren't going well or the way she wanted she would become irritable, socially withdrawn, or moody. Each time she was seen her behavior pattern was worse. This left several people that knew her puzzled, including my self. Though Jean claimed to be a born-again Christian, claimed to read her bible and to pray, she felt bad about herself. The part about feeling bad isn't too bad – we all feel that way sometimes. However, what really disturbing was that she also stated that her family didn't like her and she felt neglected - like she was the black sheep of the family. She never went into details, just that she only felt neglected and unwanted by her family members. Jean said sometimes wished she was dead.

On some occasions, in revivals that was being conducted, people were praising the Lord, Jean would start jumping up and down praising the Lord as well.

She would begin to tremble, shake, or fall backward, yelling or moaning at times. When she was finish, Jean would then run to the altar wanting to confess her unfaithfulness to God and declare her mind was really made up to serve the Lord again. After an few times of this, I really felt that she was under some kind of spell or something; an mental or emotional bondage. Did she know what it was, or where it came from?

After several years of observations of such problems as this, I was convince that this kind of bizarre behavior would required some professional evaluation and also counseling which was of course, beyond my expertise to handle. Jean was finally encourged to seek counseling from her pastor or some older church mother as quick as possible and if that didn't work, to try professional counseling. Her family knew her problems were serious, but that if she was willing to get help, then she would be closer to being healed. If Jean went to any session at all, she attended only once to my knowledge; she complained about the cost for receiving such services was the factor for not going back. Rather that was true or not, I don't know.

The older saints usually would tell me when I was young in the ministry; "Son, you can exceed at pulling a horse to the edge of the water, but you cannot make the darn horse drink." If that statement is true, then this woman's case is hereby, declare to be closed.

Now, you may consider problems of this nature an isolated incident, but it is far from that! After over twenty-five years of preaching, I have seen enough now that it posed serious questions to me, which is one of the main reasons for this book. However, a few important suggestions will be propose here to assist in resolving such problems discussed in this chapter.

Being a member of any church organization and giving services in that church does not necessary denote the presence of restoration in one's life. Nor does having sporadically, emotional outbursts with some trembling and shaking of the body guarantee that a person is fully delivered. What if the person is not sure what spirit actually touched his or her bodies? If it was the devil, that person is in big trouble now, and has not yet attained genuine spiritual restoration.

In fact, the bible says, my people are destroyed for the *lack of knowledge* - (Hosea 4:6) not the lack of the "shaking and eye fluttering symptoms" or "falling out in the aisle," especially when satan has successfully camouflaged himself into that 'person's' ecstasy emotions making them to yell, cry or whatever; in such cases, that person may not know the difference between satan or God touching them. Sometimes, people who hang around that person may not know the difference either.

Suggestions

1. You need to seek professional Christian counseling **for** deteriorated feelings or emotions that have **rob** you of your self-esteem and self-worth. Otherwise, you can look yourself in the mirror and declare," I'm going to build own self-esteem, and mean what you say.

2. Spiritual ecstasies that looked questionable may

43

need to be watched more carefully and put <u>under</u> <u>check</u> against demon infestations.
3. Families members need to sit down and <u>openly</u> <u>discuss</u> possible family curses that may have been handed down through the family line and agree to <u>form a prayer band</u> among the family membersto destroy those chains.
4. The feelings of anger and revenge built up inside of you need to be admitted and released or broken down before God and any other support services can also help.
5. Whatever prideful excuses you have need to be put aside as well - each party must become responsible for his or her own actions.

Pardon the franknes of these cases, but there are millions more of people in the same situation, whether they want to admit it or not. It is a chilling fact, and to hide or deny this means to drown in our own failures. Frankly, it is not wise.

All of the examples given in this chapter and the calamitous pile list that was mentioned earlier does differentiate from one person to another to an extent; yet, the problems stated are still imprinted upon social and church behavior even today. Nevertheless, it is important now that we move progressively toward Israel's struggle for restoration, because there are important *lessons* to be learned with this great nation as well by which all of us can seek to find anwers through which we could obtain the restoration we so badly need.

Without God, all humanity is still trapped by sin and satan's attacks and needs the transformational power of a loving Father to completely heal. Moreover, until God has a rightful place in all our lives, realistically, genuine restoration is out of the question for anyone!

Israel's quest to regain her glory and honor from past mistakes down through the centuries were not only authentic stories, but more importantly, she was the emotional soul tie. Israel is like a social dark thread tightly knitted into the fabric of our current society, which reveals the nakedness of its social, political, religions and even commercial shame. There are too many similarities between Israel and America. Did God Almighty know that history would repeat itself? Could we learn from the mistakes of others?

2 Chronicles 35: 1-27; 36:1-23

Let's look briefly at the state of the nation in (2 Chronicles, Chapters 35) under the 31 years leadership by King Josiah before moving on to Chapter 36. I want to point out the services that Josiah, as a young child king had perform that enabled this nation to enjoy a time of reformation, and blessings prior to Zedekiah's reign.

1. King Josiah tore down the idolater altars of Baalm and had them destroyed.
2. He restored the temple services and its priestly functions.
3. The Levities were ordered to teach the general population the statutes of God clearly and without fail.
4. He called for a solemn assembly of all the people

to consecrate themselves again before God.
5. Those who committed crimes were put to death.

Josiah proceeded to repair and beautify the Temple. In doing so, Hilkiah, a godly priest, found a volume (the book of Moses) which contained a copy of the judgments against disobedience on the part of the Israel, and against the defections of the nation. You can read those defections as mention in detail in the Book of Deuteronomy, (Chapters 28:15-68 and Chapter 29:16-29).

However, Josiah as a young king was profoundly moved by what he found and called for Huldah the prophetess, who declared that the punishment would surely be inflicted, but he would close his reign in peace. Josiah immediately called the people together for a solemn renewal of the covenant with God, which resulted in a religious reformation of the nation - staying the hand of destruction for 31 years. However, following the reign of Josiah, there were six kings, including Zedekiah, that drove Israel backward. There was a great exhibition of human depravity in the forms of crime, idolatry, and abominations such as Idol worshiping, gross homosexually, murder of the innocent, human sacrifice of children, and every wicked imaginations that you could think of went on.

Each king that rebelled against God would permit Babylon or Egypt to raid the city and replace one king with another. Two of the kings only had a chance to serve for a little over three months!

2 Chronicles 36:11-21 (NIV)

The question remains: was King Zedekiah a by-product of his corrupt environment, or could he be held accountable for Israel's ruins? After all, he was young - just 21 years old. Let's not make excuses for the attitudes of the officials and people he ruled. The fact is, Zedekiah's immoral life-style and his refusal to uphold righteousness did not reflect the attitudes of just his constituents. It reflected his own attitude – he was too weak, and he was too naive to the danger around him. Including him not wanted to humble himself to the advice that Jeremiah had given him. Zedekiah became stiff-necked, hardened his heart, and foolishly rebelled against King Nebuchadnezzar, and against the advice of Jeremiah.

The priest and elders carried the corruption further, even as far as to pollute the house of the Lord, which God had sanctified in Jerusalem. If that was not enough, the people began to mock Jeremiah's messages; they despised or rejected his words. Though Zedekiah privately dialogues with Jeremiah on the outcome of issues on many occasions, he simply did not want to deal with, talk out, cope with, open up, or squarely face the both his sins and those of the people. Due to such shameless denial, the nation is now in BIG trouble!

Chapter 4

The Horrible Penalties
Israel's downfall
ll Chronicles 36:11-23——Jeremiah 39:1-9

King Zedekiah of Judah, determined to hang on, knew that the siege plus a three-year famine was beginning to take its toll. Food supplies were gone, and the enemies had destroyed the water lines. Other vital supplies suddenly vanished. Frightened, he and his men decided to run for their lives.

It was dark that night of April 9th 586 B.C. when the enemies begin destroying the main gates of the city. Once inside, the soldiers burned everything. Angry soldiers went through the cities killing at will and had no compassion or sensitivity even to those who sought cover of their own temples. The invaders, like lions, trapped their prey with vehement determination. They plunged their spears and swords into the bodies of their victims while laughing and cheering with exhilaration. They watched them died in agony: the old and young men, the infirm, the disease-stricken, the virgins, the children, and even the mothers holding infants crying for mercy. The age or vulnerability of their victims did not matter to them.

The sanctuary was stripped of all great and small articles; even the treasures of God were taken. All treasures of the temple and of the king and his officers were brought to Babylon and placed in King Nebuchadnezzar's house. Other less valuable articles were destroyed or damaged. The temple itself and all its fortified buildings along with the beautiful gates were set on fire, and looked like colossal burning torches. Human bodies - some burned beyond recognition - lay scattered in the streets. It was a scene as horrific as the aftermath of the nuclear blast in Hiroshima; it was unbelievable, and too painful to see. King Zedekiah now had lost his last fortified cites - Jerusalem, Lachish and Azekah.

After the enemies left, the families, filled with anger and sorrow, began desperately digging for bodies through the ruins, around the temple area, and in the town. They continuously prayed and cried, "Oh God, let us find some of our loved ones alive!" Fortunately, they detected faint cries around the temple. "Help me, please! Somebody help!" A voice mourned. While digging, they found people buried beneath the broken wall sections of the temple with crushed legs, others far worse off, or dead. Several days passed, and stench of dead bodies was beginning to fill the air, making recovery operations unbearable. Those not accustomed to such decay odors began having vomiting spell. However, they managed to carry on with their ghastly duty.

Many of the skillful, strong, and most valued people that managed to escape from being killed were taken captive to Babylon. There they became servants to the Chaldean king and his sons for seventy years until the rule of the Kingdom of Persia, just as the prophet Jeremiah's declared. The rest of the citizens of Jerusalem that was left behind there in Jerusalem was either wounded, poverty stricken, or possessed no worthwhile skills. The Book of Daniel Chapter 12:1 reveal that those left behind during the latter part of the seven-year tribulation period would suffer conditions far worse than this.

The cloak of denial
Jeremiah 39:4-

Zedekiah, after spending several weeks in prison, could still remember that dreadful, horrifying night. They had planned an escape route, which they thought would lead them to freedom from the merciless killers racing in their direction. In his mind he could still see and hear the sound of Nergal-sharezer's voice roaring with laughter while he and his army officials stormed into Zedekiah's now empty palace. Yes, he remembered precisely how they had fruitlessly pursued an escape plan by the way of the King's gardens through the east gate which, hopefully, would lead them out of the city of Jerusalem toward Arabard. Sadly, they only made it as far as the plains of Jericho when they were spotted by the Babylonian army and then captured. The words of the prophet Jeremiah hit him like a bolt of lighting while he sat straddled like a chained animal. He sighed, "If I had only done what Jeremiah said," but now it was too late. Like a sledgehammer crashing down on his head, the dark reality for not obeying the voice of God's prophet finally hit him.

"Please drive these horrible memories away from my mind," Zedekiah pleaded in vain. He sought relief, but there was none to be found. The painful image of his sons' and noblemen's brutal murders danced before his eyes, and the memory of his humiliating dethroning by the Babylonian officers was too much to bear. His own eyes were plucked out and his face mutilated by the enemy. Was life worth living? He may have struggled with the temptation to commit suicide, but it would never happen! Jeremiah predicted that he would die peacefully and not from suicide or murder. The voice of the prophet's voice kept bringing sparks of illumination to the wilderness of his soul:

"Listen to me Zedekiah, the Lord Almighty says this: If you do not turn away from evil, I will send the people of the north, King Nebuchadnezzar, against this land and its inhabitants. I will completely destroy them and make them an object of horror and scorn, and an everlasting ruin. There they will serve the king of Babylon as slaves for seventy years."

"In fact, king, continued Jeremiah. If you would surrender to the Babylonians, which made you vassal-king in place of the rebellious Jehoiachin according to 2 King 24: 15,17

"They will not kill you or your families but will spared you. Nevertheless, if you do not surrender, they will utterly destroy you and burn this city down to nothing. Do not be persuaded by Hananiah's prophecy for it is false and he seeks only to contradict my words from the Lord God of heaven. Do not listen to him, nor, the priests, elders and trusted friends that only misled you. Obey my voice, Zedekiah, and you and your family will come out all right." Jeremiah 25:1-9 (NIV) and author's emphasis.

Zedekiah was filled with anger and guilt while remembering the prophet's words. "If only I had my eyes back again, my eyes would be like a foundation of tears." Sadly, that was out of the question. Nevertheless, the words of the prophet continued to haunt his soul like helpless prey caught in the hands of a furious animal.

I once remembered a punishment I received for something I did wrong and it was very painful. Though the punishment I got on this particular time was delayed for several days, it was only because we were notified that a guest evangelist needed to room at our home for a week, and my mother didn't want me to be embarrassed. "Oh boy," I thought, "he will be with us for a whole week and Mother will forget about the punishment, and I can go free!" As if she was reading my thoughts, my mother simply announced that she would take care of the matter later and left it at that. During the course of the long, fun week I forgot about the punishment I was to receive, but unfortunately, my mother did not. To my dismay she reminded me after the guest left. I can remember now when she would call me, "James, where are you?" She had a certain tone in her voice that would let me know I was now in big trouble. Denial, forget it. Regardless of how innocent I looked or sounded, she said it didn't work. She could recite the events perfectly while I, of course, was filled with guilt. That hurt just as bad as the belt-warming on my small bottom. In later years I thought about the correction I received from my mother and it occurred to me that God might sometimes operate in the same manner.

After all, the Lord does love us; and He will chasten you when you are wrong. Hebrew 12.6;RV. Emphasis placed.

Unfortunately, for Zedekiah and the others with him, they didn't really realize the love that God had for them, nor did God Almighty take pleasure in just allowing the enemy to run over his people. However, the warnings or brief corrections that Zedekiah was given in the past were not taken too seriously, and I don't believe our society take warnings too seriously even now!

Bankruptcies

The Babylonian raid was only the beginning of Israel's many sorrows. Fresh water and food became scarce, forcing prices for even basic necessaries to unbelievable heights. Much of the food was already spoiled. The burned forest areas left little or no resources with which to rebuild the destroyed buildings. Assassination plots and brutal fights became commonplace. No one really knew who his enemy was anymore. That meant that a good night sleep would be rare, if not impossible. Hundreds fled, taking refuge in Egypt. The rest that stayed behind would now be at the mercy of unfriendly nations boarding their towns. These forgotten, downtrodden citizens hung their heads in shame.

(Roman 6:23a) says that the wages of sin is death. Unfortunately, satan has succeeded through the centuries by casing the downfall of both Jerusalem and the entire nation of Israel, and using that nation as a continual tool of scorn and ridicule. Nevertheless, God of Heaven will one day raise them up again!

PART 2

Repentance
is
Necessary
for Restoration

Chapter 5

Going Home
Ezra 4:1-11

Thousands stood patiently not too far from the beautiful square waiting for the king and Babylonian officials to come out to make their great speech. Had news of their release from slavery somehow linked out? No one was sure. The tense and anxiety fill the air like a blanket while nervous slaves talked among themselves! The waiting crowd spotted the King and began pushing their way wildly toward the raised platform. One by one, with grim looks on their faces, the King's officials, finally mounted the platform. I wondered if the people upon hearing the good news for release began celebrating their freedom then? If they did, they had the right to. We do know that they celebrated in Jerusalem, (read Nehemiah 13th chapters). Jeremiah had remarkably prophesied that they would upon returning home, (Jeremiah 13:1-16) Perhaps, there were some who didn't believe that prophesy, however, for those who did believe it soon pay off.

The Almighty God then rise up Zerubbabel, Jeshua, and the prophet Haggai who began leading the first group of 43,000 or more Jews desiring to return to their homeland. Zerubbabel, descendant of King David, was considered a type figure of Moses, in that he is credited in leading many of the captive Jews back to the Promised Land the first time. Nevertheless, a few surprises will still await the now happy, and free, Jewish people. [1]

The horror of their past

In seeing the great stone temples in Babylon while as slaves, the now, freed Jews felt it would be a very simple thing to rebuild their own temple in the same elaborate way. Little did they know that the most important elements of their temple were the simplicity, and its spirituality of true worship that was the most essential qualities in serving their God? God wanted Haggai, the first prophet after the Jews' return to Jerusalem, conveyed to the Jewish people that it was their hearts he wanted above all and not just some big elaborate temple building. Nevertheless, every mile closer to home made the Jewish people more and more happy and excited, jumping up for joy! "We are almost home. We are almost there."

Within view of their sweet home an awful sight struck them as they glaze at the surrounding walls all looked on with uncontrollable tears and bitterness. Historically, these great *walls* and the *gates* surrounding Jerusalem were the pride and joy of their lives because they provided them protection from their enemies. Other than someone walking through with a pack on his or her back, Jerusalem looked like a ghost town. The city's landscape once filled with beautiful pine trees and myrtles were now grown over with thorn bushes and briers. Not the typical Jerusalem they had gazed upon what had once been the beautiful Solomon's Temple. It too was a devastating sight. The concrete steps were broken into thousands of pieces. The pillars of the temple were cracked and broken. The inside walls looked gloomy with black smears from their enemy's invasion seventy years earlier. The temple furnishings were broken, turned over, or had been taken away. Those who were 80 or 90 years old looked with astonishment, for they were about 15 years or older when they were taken into captivity, and so had some recollection of what the first temple had looked like then. For days on end the pessimist would only look at the ruins and cry, "Oh no! This could not have happened here!"

Could this be the same horror cry made in the streets and homes in American and elsewhere? Only this time, I believe it is people's emotional and spiritual *walls* and *gates* being crumpled.

Ezra 4: 1-16

However, Zerubbabel, along with the prophet Haggai, would not allow this distressing atmosphere to continue to dampen him or the people. "Rise up, he shouted, and let us restore this temple again!" After digging up some rusted, buried tools, their spirits began to sparkle with hope while they sat on the heaps of ruins. They began to sharpen and file their rusted edges of the tools and went to work.

Within a few years, however, the remnant that came later from Babylon met with trouble from a group of early settlers who over the seventy years had settlethere in Jerusalem. However, these people had intermarried with other nations surrounding them, prompting Zerbbabel and Jeshua refusal to allow them to help build the temple. Angry, these older settlers and their neighbors sought to weaken the hands of the workers by intimidating them or sending false accusations and letters to King Artaxeres in hopes of frighten them away from the work on the temple.

Many of the newly arrived Jews were even attacked while they worked in the fields or near the gates. The fact is, 43,000 or more newly determined Jewish people were begining to be an extreme threat to the surrounding nations now. Sadly, after a long fight with their hostile neighbors, the Jewish workers became discouraged and gave up, and was intimidated into returning to their incomplete homes in Jerusalem. The prophets Haggai had told them that the Lord wanted the house of God completed *first*. **Haggai 1:2-9** and the God of heaven would bless them. Haggai, who had gone back to Babylon for a while, returned several years later and discovered that the temple was still in deplorable

61

condition. The prophet Haggai declares to them,

Who is left among you that saw this house in her first glory? And, how do you see is now? Is it not in your eyes in comparison of it as nothing?" **Haggai 2:3**.

The prophet Haggai, is being anointed by God was called by God at an important moment in the nation's life and seeks to challenge discouraged Jews concerning the state of the temple. "

You sit in your sealed house and leave the Lord's house undone! Which of you saw this house in its first glory, and how do you see it now?"

Upon hearing the prophet's words, some of the older men sat down and began reminiscing back on the stories of King Solomon and the beautiful temple past down to them.

AndDavid had given his son, Solomon, the plans for the building the Temple of the Lord and all the surrounding rooms. He also instructed Solomon about the divisions of the priests and Leviticus, and for all the articles used in the Temples service. of this Temple as God directed him concerning the courts of the Lord.

Nevertheless, their sinful habits from the past only

seemed to take its toll on them again. They began to drift aimlessly. These up and down cycles of the people only caused the temple work to cease for several years. Interestingly, the roller coaster experiences still prevailed. The prophet *told them:*

Be strong and of good courage, and do to do the work of the Lord; fear not nor be dismayed: for the Lord God, even my God, will be with thee; he will not fail thee, nor forsake thee, until though has finished all the work for the service of the Temple.

Problems worsen when the native Jews began to marry members of the idolatrous neighboring nations: namely, the Ammonites, Moabites, Emeritus, and Egyptians. The people's worship and obedience to the laws of God became more designative. Not only was this prevalent among the common people, but the princes and rulers, *"had been chief in this trespass* **Ezra** 9:2.[3] As a result, the responsibilities of the temple were neglected, the singing choir discontinued their joyful songs on the Sabbath, and the Levites declared an end to reading the laws of Moses. And, for some bewildering reason, the Priest finally canceled all worship services. The mingling with the people of the surrounding lands pulled Israel back into the same condition it had been in years earlier

Who will stand in the Gap?
There in the Holy of Holiness, the high priest would enter alone once a year on the Day of Atonement,

and sprinkle the blood of the offering upon the mercy-seat. The yearly sacrifices were a solemn occasion through which the priest would offer the sacrifices for the sins of the nation. As the representative of the people, the priests were only allowed into this sacred room.

Sadly, during the reign of Zedekiah and also the interval between Zerubbabel and the coming of the High priest, Ezra, the priests that served stood unqualified to officiate those services. Perhaps the priest, being conscious of its corrupt life, would fear the wrath of God would come upon him, thus, would **avoided** entering the place of the Holy of Holiness.

Ezra's 9th chapter

The Jews did manage to complete the temple. However, for the next 58 years, up to the coming of Ezra, the normal operations of the temple played out. These people appeared to being without any strong spiritual representation in the city. They continued to pay tribute to the Persian crown, but the governing power was fickle. As far as the civil and criminal laws were concerned, these Jewish people did what seemed good in their own eyes. [2] As it says:

The way of a foolish person is right in his or her own eyes, but he that harkened or listen unto counsel is wise.

Therefore, it was important that a new, dedicated priest like Ezra be place again in this office so that the nation is reestablished. Thus, we see through the significance of this religious system, symbolizing the way of approach to God by means of expiation, propitiation by the mercy seat, God's presence with his people and as well as their communion with him.

The Law's limitations

A close search of the institutional laws found in the books of Exodus, Deuteronomy, Leviticus, and also, book of Numbers clearly show the people in the beginning had a well-organized system to work with.

The laws, totaling more than 600, were divided into three main categories; **(1)** *Moral,* **(2)** *Ceremonial,* and **(3)** *Judicial,* with the greater parts of these laws being devoted to ceremonial regulations. Sometimes, the laws couldbe referred to as: principles rules, or the book of Moses. Nevertheless, these Jewish people failed to understand the true purpose of the laws; though the law were good, just that the law itself were not the means to salvation, but **stood instead as a shadow to better things to come.**
Hebrews 10:1. In fact, two of these laws particular would typify the office work of the *coming Messiah* priesthood and sacrifice.

> *The Lord has sworn, and will not revoke or change it: YOU are a **Priest forever** after the manner and order of Melchizedek. **(Psalms 110:4); (Hebrew 5:10; 7:11,15,21).** Author's rendered.*

Throughout the history of the Jewish people, the Divine

65

substance that was being prepared for them was not understood or they made have simply ignored it. And, yes, it was predictable.

*For the LORD hath poured out upon you the spirit of deep sleep, and hath closed your eyes: the prophets and your rulers, the seers hath he covered. And the vision of all is come unto you as the words of a book that is sealed, which men deliver to one that is learned, saying, Read this, I pray thee: and he said, I cannot; for it is sealed: **Isaiah 29:10-11**.* Author emphasis.

There are 34 prophecies made in regard to the life and work of the Messiah, beginning in the book of **Genesis 3:15 and** ending at **Malachi 3:1-6.** More than 60 quotations or references were in the Old Testament concerning the Coming Messiah. Isaiah made more than 25 quotations alone!

*For what the **law could not do**, in that it was weak through the flesh, God sending His own Son in the likeness of sinful flesh, and for sin, condemned sin in the flesh.* **Roman 8:3.** Author emphasis.

Even with the best of efforts, Jewish people along with any other will *only fail* to show God through their merits and good works how good they were to his acceptance.

The law, if fail even in just one point- *read Roman 7:4-25,* would produce misery and would follow us like a shadowy ghost forcing one to see its sinful natures more and recognize how hopelessly one is without

66

God's mercy and grace. Including the fact, no one could depend on to any institutions that teaches against, or contradict the person of Christ Jesus as the Son of God, who is the only one that could deliver us from the _curse_ of the law.

8 The Scripture foresaw that God would justify the Gentiles by faith, and announced the gospel in advance to Abraham: "All nations will be blessed through you."
9 So those who have faith are blessed along with Abraham, the man of faith.
10 All who rely on observing the law are under a curse, for it is written: "Cursed is everyone who does not continue to do everything written in the Book of the Law."
11 Clearly no one is justified before God by the law, because, "The righteous will live by faith."
12 The law is not based on faith; on the contrary, "The man who does these things will live by them."
13 Christ redeemed us from the curse of the law by becoming a curse for us, for it is written: "Cursed is everyone who is hung on a tree."
14 He redeemed us in order that the blessing given to Abraham might come to the Gentiles through Christ Jesus, so that by faith we might receive the promise of the Spirit.
Gal 3:8-14 (NIV)

The Work of the Coming Christ

*For unto us a **child** is born, unto us a **son** is given: and the government shall be upon His shoulder: and his name shall be called Wonderful, Counselor, The mighty God, The everlasting Father, The Prince of Peace.*

*The increase of His government and peace there shall be no end, upon the throne of David, and upon **His kingdom,** to order it, and to establish it with judgment and with justice from henceforth-even **forever**. The zeal of the LORD of hosts will perform this.* **Isaiah 9:6-7.** Authors' emphasis

*He is despised and rejected of men; a man of sorrows, and acquainted with grief: and we hid as it were our face from Him; He was **despised**, and we esteemed him not.*

*Surely He **hath borne** our grief, and **carried** our sorrows: yet we did esteem Him stricken, smitten of God, and afflicted.*

*But He was **wounded** for our transgressions, He was **bruised** for our iniquities: the **chastisement** of our peace was upon Him; and with we are healed.*

*All we like sheep have **gone astray**; we have turned everyone to his own way; and the LORD hath laid on Him (Messiah) the iniquity of us all.*

*He **(The Lamb of God)** was oppressed, and he was afflicted, yet He opened not his mouth: He is brought as a lamb to the slaughter, and as a sheep before her*

Shearer is dumb, so He opened not his mouth. **Isaiah 53:1-7.** Author's emphasis

The laws along with its Mosaic institutions were good for the dispensation of which it was ordained to work and it does hold many interesting significances, like the Mercy-Seat, Ark of the Covenant, Vail of the temple, etc; all of these will show us in the sense of revelation, the type figure of Christ.

Nevertheless, the bible also clearly will prove, particularly book of Hebrew, that:

1. The Jewish law was only a *schoolmaster* to bring all people into the saving power of Jesus Christ.

2. The out ward Moasic institutions and appointments provided fail and could not provide restoration that all humanity really needed today.

3. Faith in the sacrifical work of Christ Jesus on the cross of Calvary was and still is the requiremnet for salvation, both, to the Jew and Gentiles alike.

4. Jesus Christ, the Son of God is the mediator between God, his Father,and man and, also, Jesus 'Christ stands as the fulfiller of the New Covenant to the Jewish people and Christians around world for both the Old and New Testament.

Chapter 6

"Lord, Revive us again!"

Ezra, famous priest, teacher of the law, was commissioned by King Artaxerxes to teach the laws of God in Jerusalem. He, along with seven advisers and 1496 more Jewish men journey to Jerusalem thirteen years before Nehemiah, around 458 B.C. This was in the seventh year of King Artaxerxes's rule, a critical moment in Jewish people's history. Zerubbabel and Joshua, two great men who had served in the past had passed on and there was no one readily available to provide the same high standard of leadership as these men. The Jewish people spiritual life had greatly degenerated over the last fifty years, caused by the people's lack of observing the laws of God that had governed their lives in the past. [1]

The coming of Ezra as the new priest and teacher provided new hope for restoration for the dispirited people. Like the prophet Samuel, Ezra ministry seemed to flow in the same manner. However, Ezra roles were limited to that of a priest, and teacher of the law, while Nehemiah came on later as the governor and builder of the *wall* and *gates*. Nevertheless, Ezra realized that being the man of the hour for that task he would have to work hard in restoring the divine place of worship and set out speedily to put the temple services back in order. [2] In fact, Ezra proficient as a teacher may have done more to help make Nehemiah's later services as governor and builder with Jerusalem easier.

Setting the House in order

The first thing Ezra did when he reached Jerusalem was to pray and confess the sins of his people. Ezra knew the only way the temple services and the nation could be restored was by reestablishing the people's obedience and loyalty to the divinely ordained institutions that had regulated their lives. [3]

Our forefathers, who founded America centuries ago, like the Jewish nation, knew this as well. And, with what knowledge they had to work with, they set out to establish our religious structure using governmental prototype similar to those of the Jewish nations; particular, the judicial and moral laws. These laws gave our forefathers inspiration, contributed much to the sovereign and blessings they enjoyed then. Americans are barely grasping the same principals our fore fathers lay down today.

Interestingly, the Jewish people saw nothing less but prosperous days as long they kept the commandants. Naturally, I do understand that those Mosaic laws were just the prototype of the Divine Savior. However, for that period, they did serve as a guiding light and bridge to all the blessings God had for them. Prophetically speaking, there is a spiritual significance in these regulations as noted in **(John 8:12-58)**, which may hold clues to the dilemmas facing us today.

Repentance is necessary

Ezra remembered the prayer that Solomon prayed to God in that temple, and the response that God gave back to Solomon. Ezra, a powerful priest, clearly stood qualified to bring a revival to the hearts of people. The bible says...

He prepared himself to seek the law of the Lord, and to teach in Israel statutes and judgments? **Ezra 7:10.**

Ezra prayers were so impressive that the people were profoundly moved. Success for restoration would need to involve the nations confession or admitting the wrong done, and a repentant spirit in turning away from that wrong done while seeking the face of the Almighty. This act of repentance would help to ensure the temple services being renewed and Gods people being rightfully secured again.

Whenever a nation like Israel ignores its moral

72

and spiritual obligations to God, its relationship with God becomes damaged. Consequently, it becomes *blinded* by false hopes and purposes, and becomes *ensnared* in its irrational errors. These errors eventually cause economic, social, and spiritual hardships, much as they did in Jerusalem.

The important question comes to mind? Why does mankind not learn through the past mistakes of Jewish peoples? Of course, I gladly give thanks to the pioneers and current leaders who have fought hard for the standards of living now enjoy by many. However, since the birth of our nation, there has been a great change in the structure and thinking of our nation and world in the last twenty-five years, our social, economic and spiritual structures are increasing in chronic proportions and cannot be corrected merely by intellectual methods. America needs a national spiritual awakening in which the church and government need to confess and repent of personal and corporate sins.

We must also remember that God has always been willing to provide and sustain us. He delights in blessing His people with material blessings and health; however, these blessings do not come without a corresponding spiritual obligation, and a repentant heart for turning away from the God of heaven and His holy Word!

ANeed to Return
According to Dr. Henry C. Link, a famous psychologist and writer explained the significance of the

Christian religion as exemplified by the social aggressiveness of its population. There is an absence of emphasis on forgetting oneself in the service of others. Religion had been one merely of *believing certain things* rather than one of *commitment to godly works* or love of service.

Dr. C. Link goes on to say that, *"selfishness* leads to *greed,* greed to temptation for criminal behavior, from that, to the state of *denial* of ones guilt. American ideology has leaded the country into an era of prodigality in which we feel science is greater than religious truths and our reasoning is better than moral values. It is true that American discovery of scientific breakthroughs allows a more comfortable life, medical discovery for better health, and a life filled with an infinite variety of technology for better communication and faster transportation. "Yet, with all of this advancement of our culture offers **no evidence** that individuals are being made happier, that families stay together longer, that governments or political agencies are wiser in balancing the budget or resolving major problems. Nor do scientific breakthroughs make world communities show genuine respect for one another." Evidence to such claim tends to point to the contrary. [4]

The price tag for straying away
Hosea 6:1 Come, and let us return unto the Lord:
The chosen people were urged by the prophet Hosea to return to God or suffer the consequences. The

case is the same with America and other nations as well today. Recently reports show that many believe we may be sitting on a self-obliterating bomb as the modern, developing countries tussles with its crime and corruption problems. For an example:

America suffers the highest violent crime rate of any nation in the world, according to the Criminal Justice Institutes 1996 Corrections Yearbook.

In 1977, Anthony G. White, a writer, provided this special report, entitled: Restitution As A Criminal Sentence.

The increase of crime, especially in urban areas, has strained the corrections systems of urban areas and urban states to the limit. Jails and prisons are full, halfway houses are overcrowded, and other confinement facilities are equally overtaxed. Many convicted individuals who 20 years ago who would have been incarcerated are today set free on probation because there is no room for them.

Such situations have forced the creation of innovative techniques to control convicted people while at the same time attempting to rehabilitate them. Among these newly adopted techniques, coupled with probation, is the concept of restitution.

Financial restitution involves payment by the criminal for property losses, damages, or medical bills to the victim of the crime. If a loss can be documented then the courts may be inclined to order restitution as condition of the criminal's probation. Symbolic restitution, where a dollar amount cannot be determined in a crime (such as for the pin and indignity of being subjected to am criminal act) can involve doing public service to "work off" the "debt" to the victim or to society.

The theory is that the criminal redeems himself/herself by sharing the suffering or loss of the victim, and the victim is in turn relieved of any financial burden brought about by the crime. The process is also supposed to increase interpersonal understanding between the criminal and victim, using the criminal justice system as a referee.

Two drawbacks are immediately apparent to the concept. First, such a "punishment" may convince criminals that they can commit crimes that, if caught, they can buy their way out of at a later date. Second, it is unknown whether any rehabilitative effects are generated by requiring such payments of an individual who probably has little money and few job prospects.

Research is now being carried on throughout the nation through funding by the Law Enforcement Assistance Administration to determine the rehabilitative impact of restitution as a sentence. Whatever the results, one thing is certain: the bibliographic list of relevant literature will be much larger in a few years than it is today.[5]

Base on the report of Mr. White the crime statistics shown

will categorically prove that Mr. Anthony G. White fear of failure with *"Restitution as criminal sentence"* program was indeed correct. Not only have crime rate gone up, but also criminal behavior is worse.

One violent crime was committed every 19 seconds in 1996 as compared to 38 seconds in 1972, one murder was committed every 27 minutes. Aggravated assault was committed against someone every 31 seconds in 1996 as compared to 84 seconds in 1972. Somebody's business or home was burglarized every 13 seconds in 1996. There are more than 1,191 million divorces each year in America.

In 1980, there were 401,786 adults incarcerated. In 1993 there were 1,304,686 million inmates with the greatest population being males.

In 1996 there were 1,030,888 million arrests made from drug abuse violations compared to 654,426 in 1987. That is about a 57.5% increase!

For teens less than 18 years of age: 61,358 arrest were made in 1987; in 1996 there were 142,922 arrests. That's 132.9% change![6]

The current decade shows an alarming concern about hate crimes, Congress, on April 23, 1990, enacted the Hate Crime Statistics Act of 1990.

Out of 10,702 reported offenses, racial bias led the

top by reported 6,768 cases. Religious bias came in with 1,497 report cases follow by 1,258 with sexual-orientation bias, and 1,179 with ethnic bias complaints.[7] We understanding that this trend of crime does go up and down from year to year. Nevertheless, the institute says overall, the social behavior in places like America is not getting any better, but worse!

The tragedies from terrorist acts like the one in the Oklahoma City federal building in April 1995, and the Branch Davidian compound near Waco, Texas, in of April 1993 should be a wakeup call that America may be facing more future sieges.

Dr. Larry B. Silver says that the suicide rate *has tripled* in the past 30 years. The bulk of suicide occurs in the 20-24 year old age groups, but the *15-19* year olds also at risk.

The American Psychiatric Association estimates that each year 5,500 teenagers commit suicide. Most all cases of suicide stem from prolonged depression. [8] I do believe that most of these suicides and tragedies with insanity could have been prevented if these people had come to know and accept Jesus as Lord and Savior of their lives.

Our nation leads the world as a purveyor of pornography. According to *Adult Video New*, an industry trade publication, the number of hard-core video rentals rose from 75 million in 1985 to 490 million in 1992. The total climbed to 665 million, an all-time high, in 1996. Last year, Americans spent more than $8 billion on hard-core videos, peep shows, live acts, adult cable programming, sexual devices, computer porn, and sex a magazines-an amount much larger than Hollywood domestic box office receipts and larger than all the revenues generated by rock and country music recordings. Americans now spend more money at strip clubs than at Broadway, off-Broadway, regional, nonprofit theaters at the opera, ballet, and jazz and classical music performances combined. [9]

" Scandal fever has taken over," says political scientist Larry J. Sabato. "Years ago, you get one good scandal every few years. Now it is scandal dujour."

Suzanne Garment, in her 1991 book, *Scandal:* "The Crisis of Mis-Trust in American Politics," observed that unprecedented number of public scandals erupted in the fifteen years after the botched Watergate cover-up drove Richard Nixon from the Presidency in 1974. Garment counted more than 400 relatively senior federal officials and candidates for federal office who have been publicly accused in the National press of personal wrongdoing" during those fifteen years. The question is, are we more corrupted? According to political reformers in the press, public-interest advocacy groups, the new law and regulations that forced executive branch agencies to make many more of their internal records available to the public and press has not helped much. The number of our political scandals has continually increased. [10]

One look at these statistics, and we should admit that the social fabrics of America are rapidly breaking down. The gates of our economic, political and spiritual well being of our society are burning with the desires of obnoxious attitudes and discontent. The streets of America bear witness to this. There is a sense of hopelessness in our homes and doom in our schools, and indifference in our churches.

The above-mentioned statistics are not getting any better. The Associated Press released this poll on June 15, 1997. More than half of Americans consider racism an intractable dilemma that president can control. [14] Ninety out of hundred people expressed to me they believe America and the world is **hostage** to its own fears, **confused** abut its destiny, **ensnared** by its political and social mistakes, **entrapped** by its wealthy, smart criminals, and **bled financially by parasites.** Those who show little interest in church say that the church in their communities is different from what it was twenty years ago, and it doesn't meet the needs of people that are hurting. We know there is a church that can help them, but, they are under such demonic stronghold that it will take a miracle from God's power to save them.

A sample polling of the youth over the years tells us there is an impoverishment of values and they think the world, and especially their parents, owes them a living. They admit they enjoyed *hanging out*, and seem to lack a sense of responsibility. Due to limited parental rights, many of the parents have to almost beg or pay their kids to go to church. As a children growing up, my mother would just look at us, we knew at 9:00 a.m. sharp, to be ready to go to Sunday School, no questions ask. Be careful with that... "Mom, I don't want go to Sunday School," message on my face. That may spell trouble! Now that I think about it, my mother trying to raise eight children alone was quite a challenge. Even though she was firm with us many times, mother's firm, but loving hands with her children eventual pay off.

The teens go on to say their main objective in life is to have fun, and their idea of a good time, so far as most of us can see, is doing what want they want to do. Apparently that freedom has been allowed, which may have account for half of the nation's crime rate. If allowed to continue such behavior, they will become a **self-destruct** weapon again themselves and as well as against others. This includes being a misfit in society. Such a kind of person seems to lack the less in life enrichment.

People like, Dr. Laurence Jones, founder of Piney Woods County School, in Mississippi, Dr. Shirley Chisholm, Congresswoman and civil rights activist; Rev. Billy Graham, a renowned crusade speaker, and many others emerge from their hard work, discipline of character. And, it is widely agreed, that they experienced a happier life both spiritually and naturally,

81

but knew the path to obtain this type of life as well. They though more highly of their fellow man, and have acquired greater confidence in themselves. Naturally or spiritually, godly people of character under long but satisfied pressure have learned that love of service is more satisfying than introspection, and hard, honest physical work sweeter than self-indulgence.

These great leaders emerge from the cotton gin or humble ways of life better equipped to give their energies and attention to others and therefore were more appreciative to the reward of services given.[11]

They're only a fraction of the outstanding people founded who stood as giants ready to rebuild broken walls and burned gates in America. They were like Nehemiah and many others, dedicated and courageous in their task, and stood as a good example of those willing to give their lives for the benefit of humanity if necessary. As mentioned before, and will be explained again in more detail later, Israel failure to follow the prophets of God as being the root cause of their national woes. As you study each chapter, look for clues around your own backyards and communities. I believe you, like Nehemiah and Ezra, will begin to find answers in prayer.

Part 3

Restorational Builders
Past and Present

Chapter 7

The Divine Call

Nehemiah, a famous reformer came to Jerusalem in 445 B.C. thirteen years after Ezra as an appointed governor. According to history, his father, name, Hacaliah and family were members of the tribe of Judah. And, apparently they belonged to the *Jews of the dispersion*, that is, persons scattered abroad. [1] As a lad growing up in Babylon during the captivity period he was some how ushering into the Persia Court where he soon founded approbation with the king and queen. And for the next several years, Nehemiah served faithfully his duties as a *cupbearer*, that is, Mashgiah, meaning one giving drink. This was a very important job that required skill and trustworthiness. His proficient may have landed him larger responsibility in training and supervising others servants as need. It was not uncommon to receive such favor as with the case of Prophet Daniel who was surname,

Bel-teshazzar during the reign of King Cyrus, Esther in the reign of King Ahasuerus, many others. Remember, when God wants to change circumstances he doesn't need anybody permission to do so; he can simply do it because he is God of the universeBy the time Nehemiah had finish his assignments as a cupbearer with the Persia Court he had developed and almost perfect the nesccary skill.

Historically, he is considered a man of remarkable productivity, and admirable dedication. His ability to go up against supreme odds, and unshakable faith is inspirational. Some of these charismatic flavors seen in this great man stem from his patriotism for his people and the historical Jewish training he had received through godly parents.

Nehemiah obviously was a man of devotion to God Almighty and spent great deal of time in prayer. In the secular sense, he was better off financially than most Jewish people could have been engrossed in his own worldly success rather than be concerned about the conditions in Jerusalem. However, the descriptions of Jerusalem and its glorious past meant more to him than all the riches or success he could attain in Babylon. He was willing to give it all up and suffer affliction with the people of God, than enjoy the pleasures of Babylon.

Finding renewal through prayer

Nehemiah's chambers offered him a private and quiet spot where he could steal away for a period of meditation and prayer. It was often in this type of solitude that God developed and prepared great leaders for great tasks, and it may hold true even today.   I realize that the complexity of our time will not afford us the same type offsetting as the prophets of old. However, we can be creative for the sake of our spiritual well being. Try hunting or fishing trip, or a walk along the walking trails. Try something, anything worthwhile. Have a heart for your mental sanity and tight nerves. You are the one that need to hear from God.

The Prayer Chambers

When his brother Hanani shared with Nehemiah about the condition of the dismantled Holy city and the affliction borne upon the Jews he was devastated. Yet he prayed.

4 When I heard these words I sat down and wept, and mourned for days, fasting and praying before the God of heaven.   Neh 1:4 (NRSV)

How long this pray and fasting period lasted heaven only knows. One thing is certain he knew that things were at critical point and he couldn't stop until he got a answer from God.

Note following prayer of Nehemiah:

5 I said, "O LORD God of heaven, the great and awesome God who keeps covenant and steadfast love with those who love him and keep his commandments; 6 Let your ear be attentive and your eyes open to hear the prayer of your servant that I now pray before

you day and night for your servants, the people of Israel, confessing the sins of the people of Israel, which we have sinned against you. Both my family and I have sinned.

7 We have offended you deeply, failing to keep the commandments, the statutes, and the ordinances that you commanded your servant Moses.

8 Remember the word that you commanded your servant Moses, 'If you are unfaithful, I will scatter you among the peoples;

9 But if you return to me and keep my commandments and do them, though your outcasts are under the farthest skies, I will gather them from there and bring them to the place at which I have chosen to establish my name.'

10 They are your servants and your people, whom you redeemed by your great power and your strong hand.

11 O Lord, let your ear be attentive to the prayer of your servant, and to the prayer of your servants who delight in revering your name. Give success to your servant today, and grant him mercy in the sight of this man!" At the time, I was cupbearer to the king. Neh 1:4-11 (NRSV)

It is clear by this prayer of Nehemiah that he was aware of how Jewish nation had been brought out of Egypt by the great power of God and literally processes the riches of the Canaanites, the Amorites, the Hittites, the Perizzites, the Hivites, and the Jebusites. However, he also knew that in order for his people to enjoy such level of restoration like that again they would need the presence of God in their mist. Note carefully the words spoken by God and Moses in Exodus 33:14-17 (NIV)

14 The LORD replied, "My Presence will go with you, and I will give you rest."
15 Then Moses said to him, "If your Presence does not go with us, do not send us up from here.
16 How will anyone know that you are pleased with me and with your people unless you go with us? What else will distinguish me and your people from all the other people on the face of the earth?"

Since Nehemiah knew about Moses, could he have reflected on these same words of Moses as well? Could they have been the very groundwork by which he develops his prayer life? We are merely left to speculate; nevertheless, this amiable man reveals a striking character in revelation that is immense with scripture and certainly is a good pattern for all who wish to follow.

Now, with this desire and pray in mind he elude temptations that led toward personal self-exaltation, self-dependence, or a worldly lifestyle. He knew that such a state of mind would only cause a loss of all sense of his need for God and whatever spiritual advantages' God had bestowed on him. After all, as Moses requested the presence of God for success of restoration, Nehemiah felt the same need if not more. Without it he would be just spinning his wheels going nowhere.

Find God in Prayer

Like Nehemiah, believers seeking for restoration today should seek equally to maintain daily their spiritual intimacy with God in prayer and should while praying anticipate three goals in prayer. First, that they <u>may hear</u> what God is saying in an intellectual manner.

Second, they <u>would feel</u> the emotional intensity of what God is saying to them while in prayer.

Thirdly, that they would <u>be convinced</u> in the mind that he (God) is right and line up with the Word of God accordingly. Only when these prayer goals have been properly assimilated will we become the essence of what God is looking for and complete the process of restoring lives wherever it is needed.

A interview with Governor Nehemiah

Let's build a *scenario case* involving a mental interview with Governor Nehemiah and let see what he may share with us on prayer.

Suppose you were the one interviewing Nehemiah on *NBC Nightly News...*

"I must tell you, Mr. Nehemiah, people around the world admire your character and effective leadership skill. If you have a few moments, sir, I like to interview you."

"Please tell me what you feel that contributed to your

success in life the most."

The governor voice chuckles as he prepares to answer.
"Well, a strong prayer life, of course. Beside that, faith in the Word of God."

"How do you define prayer for one's life, the interviewer ask him."

" Let's see, he look solemnly at the cheering crowd. To me, prayer becomes the most powerful form of energy generated from the heart of the petitioner. It is a force as real as terrestrial gravity, pulling down the favor of God toward humankind. Also, the radium of that prayer will produce the important source of luminous, self-g"That so powerful, sir," exclaims the young interviewer. By this time the young interviewer's spirit is beginning to boil with excitement and chills seem to tickle down its spine.

"Nevertheless, sir, why do *you* pray?"

The governor looked at the young interviewer, and with a smile of concern, he answered.

"Frankly, I pray to *link my self* with the inexhaustible motivational power that spins the universe. For many years I have been confident that God Almighty would apportion this power to my needs, as I trusted him. Even in asking, I find the power of God Almighty fills my human deficiencies and I arise strengthened and repaired to finish the work of restoration."

"I am proud to say, sir, you have always been a mentor to me, says the interviewer, almost losing its posture. The supreme odds you and the faithful workers had to go up against in restoring Jerusalem is remarkable. You

90

deserve a place in the *Guinness Book of Records.*"

"Thank you, I appreciate the confidence you have in my life and pray for great success in your life as well."

"Governor Nehemiah, I have another question to ask you before you go." In brief, can you expand an little more to us, sir, what do you believe sincere prayer would do for humankind now?"

The amiable governor then scratches his head as if he was trying to sum up words. Suddenly, his eyes and face sparkle. "Well, when humankind addresses God almighty in fervent prayer, they change both soul and body for better. They also will invite the power of the Almighty God to flow through their lives for restoration. Then, they can become instrument of deliverance themselves and for other people's lives."[2]

You are in the making

Even though our skills and abilities may not be as great as Nehemiah and may vary from one person to another. Yet, there lies in all Christians some potential unknown skills to some, to lead out in something great: whether it is in religious matters, political, business oriented, or just at home. God, who is the master of our lives often will start the developing process of those skills and abilities to be brought to maturity as result of some good, and oh yes, bad experience that he graciously brings us through. Even if most of those experiences are our fault they work out God plans and will bring us to a point where He can use us as a blessing to others, as well as to ourselves later in life.

For some, it may be difficult to fully comprehend what Paul declared:

28 We know that all things work together for good for those who love God, who are called according to his purpose. Romans 8:28 (NRSV)

It took me year with bizarre occurrences, indecisive moments at the cross road to fully understand what Paul says in above verse. In fact, some of the ordeals would leave me wondering how long, or why me? But, by studying the Book of Nehemiah, it's inspirational to see this servant persistent in the face of trial and keep an open mind as to God's will for his life. By studying his patterns it was much easier for me to assimilate my own thought patterns and better cogitated what taking place. At the same time, it is very possible that one can allow their minds to become close to the thing of God. In fact, several of the people I counseled within the past had done this and as a result, they did not understand what God was saying to them either directly or through another spokesperson. Now, their growth has become stunted, and they never seen to progress in the things of God.

8 For my thoughts are not your thoughts, nor are your ways my ways, says the LORD.
9 For as the heavens are higher than the earth, so are my ways higher than your ways and my thoughts

than your thoughts. Isaiah 55:8-9 (NRSV)

What the writer is saying is that God's character and mannerisms cannot be *totally* understood because our perception of him is limited, just like a child or baby does not understand his parents. However, we must *develop* and nurture our trust in God, and depend on his promissory note (the Word of God) to lead us in the right direction when we obey him. What He says and what He does can be puzzling, but after a while He will unfold the secret as we become mature to go forth from day to day.

Chapter 8

Restoring the Wall and Gates

Nehemiah (2:12, 15, 16)

Let's visualize in our minds Nehemiah's 700 miles trip to Jerusalem. According to the scriptures he had brought only a few military men for protection and to carry needed supplies. Approaching outer parts of the city, the appointed governor decides to sit on the side of a slope not far from the city walls and rest awhile. While resting he probably had a chance to admire the most beautiful scene of which he had long heard about in Babylon. The flowers dotting the area filled the air with a sweet fragrance while creating a magnificent feeling within him. Glancing around, he decided to stop the group that had traveled with him there while he could go little farther somewhere alone to pray. Walking a distance, he fell on his face and began pray.

"Oh God, my Father, thank you for bringing us safe this far. I am here, and now in need of your divine guidance's. Show me what I must do next. For the enemies of my people are very strong and Sanballat the Horonite, and Tobiah his servants and the Ammonite people will stop at nothing to destroy the efforts for prosperity and peace. "Guide me, thou great Jehovah."

The answer from God of heaven began pouring into his mind. Confident of God's guidance, Nehemiah surveyed the city walls and gates alone by night, and rested and planned during the day. He was well aware of Sanballat's shrewd ability to attack him and the citizens and naturally, fear of his coming was a serious concern. Furthermore, knowledge the exact time for arrival would encourage Sanballat to fashion clever ploys, which would make repair projects more difficult. Besides, Nehemiah needed time and space to consider things. Already, there is too much skepticism in the city and the morale was down. "A pure anointing from the arm of the Lord would be needed to complete this project. After the three-day survey, he could now meet with city officials laying out strategies by which restoration of the nation's wall and gates could began. For the wall and gates repairs was vital to the Jewish people well being, and without it, the country's future weighted in the balance.

It is in this chapter that we like to examine the physical look of those gates and enjoining wall as well as the spiritual aspect of restoring the gates and wall in the new church age. There are many Old Testament scriptures that support the natural and also the spiritual uses of the wall and gates, and yet, there are more to be revealed in the New Testament as well. Let's see what we will find?

The significance of the Gates

The word *"gate"* comes from a Hebrew word, *sha'sr,* meaning an opening that is, the entrance or opening. The word gates are referred to more than 39 times in the Old Testament and 9 times in the New Testament, all which use the language of gates both metaphorically and in a natural sense. In the natural sense the gate or gates were the main entrances to enclose buildings, grounds, and in Jerusalem's case, their cities. We must stress here that the gates and wall often three important things:

1. Distinctive of the nation's character
2. Opportunity for profitableness in marketing products
3. The gates was where the nations social, spiritual, and political matter was dealt with.
4. The wall and gates would provide protection from the enemies and boundaries rights.

The Gates diminished glory
Listed here are the dismantled gates and enjoining walls' mention in **Nehemiah Chapter 3: 2-32.**

Sheep gate, Fish gate, Horse gate, Gate of the Fountain, Dung gate, Water gate, Valley gate, East gate/golden gate, Gate Miphkad, Old Gate.

Of course, if you may have already read chapter four where the Babylonian army came against Israel and destoryed the wall and sat fire to her gates in 586 B.C. Read that chapter again if necessary. What is so crucial with that story is, satan desired to use the same principal and approach, except it is our emotional wall and gates he is after.

Our mind, being the most pliant part of our body, serves as the point of entrance for demons to come in. If allowed-that is, the gates left unguarded, he can and will influence the thoughts, idea, and feeling patterns within us. Remember in chapter two where I talked about the lack of restoration- that is a good example there. Therefore, to prevent satan's control, there must be a suitable and systematically pattern in directing one's thoughts and meditation toward heavenly ideas, according to Isaiah.

I will keep you in perfect peace whose mind is steadfast,

because you trust in me. (Isaiah 26:3)

Otherwise, if you don't strive to keep your focus on Christ the enemy of our souls would inflict the mind with confusion if given the chance to do so.

In the next few pages, I will underscore a few examples of the significance of these emotional and spiritual gates in our lives.

Figuratively speaking, the Bible has much to say about the gates. For example: *To prossess the gates* could also mean to prossess the city as well, (Genesis 22:17; 24:60) and for obvious reasons the soldiers wuld shut the gates at nightfall and reopen them in the morning.

The securing of the gates stood as the wellbeing of a city-see (Isaiah 3:26; 14:31 and Jeremiah 14:2). David referred to the word gates a number of times to express or draw upon its meaning in the both the natural and metaphorically.

(Psalm 24:7,9) Lift up your heads, O you gates; and be lifted up, you age-abiding doors; and the King of glory shall come in.

God promise Abraham a blessing that included his *possessing the gates* of his enemies.

That in blessing I will bless thee, and in multiplying I

will multiply thy seed as the stars of the heaven, and as the sand, whichis upon the seashore; and thy see shall possess the gate of his enemies; (Gen. 22:17)

Here in below passage of scripture the Jewish people 's very lives stood as the metaphorical *entrance* or *doorway* through which the glory of God passes. God wanted his people to experience the harmony, beauty and refinment of His Spirit within as well as enjoy the natural success without. Then David change the picture somewhat to included the picture of the emotional gates into gates of righteousness in (Psalms 118:19-24)

Open for me the gates of righteousness; I will enter and give thanks to the LORD. This is the gate of the LORD through whichthe righteous may enter. I will give you thanks, for you answered me; you have become my salvation. the LORD has done this, and it is marvelous in ur eyes. This is the day the LORD has made; let us rejoice and be glad in it.
(Psalm 118:19-24)

In (Psalm 100:4) We now enter the *gates* of the Almighty God- that is, a place where God desires to inhabited with his own people. There we bow down to worship and then we raise up to praise Him until His glory fill our bodies in the same manner it filled the courtyard with Ezekiel.

Moreover, the glory of the LORD entered the temple by the gate or place of entrance, facing the east. (Ezekiel 43:4).

What agreement is there between the temple of God and idols? for we are the temples of the living God as God has said: "I will live with them and walk among them, and I will be their God, and they will be my people." (2 Cor. 6:16) NIV.

In the spiritual sense, our bodies can now take on the formost area of being the courtyard and as well as the temple where the God of glory desires to dwell within.

You will keep in perfect peace him whose mind is steadfast, because he trusts in you. (Isaiah 26:3) (NIV)

Improper judgment

One of the most common mistakes we made is from judgment or decisions made for either a family's well-being, church programs, personal health and/or career goals. The spirit of confusion usually will bring on this lack of good judgment and will bring destruction if the problem is not check in time. This will happen when the gates of our minds is left open to demons and they will simply block spiritual hearing so that you are not clearly hearing or knowing what God is saying about our lives, possessions or motives.

(Proverbs 3:5) says in all your ways acknowledge him.

Solomon says in all of our ways, which takes in every facade of our life. Honestly, we fail in this area sometime? We think we know what is best, and the truth with the above scripture with us is, God knows that we are prone sometime is to tuning Him out of our lives. The only way we find out that He was *right* is when we have made a total wreck in doing things our way for a while. In cases such as these, God is not the cause of the consequence we suffer from our mistakes. We must bear full responsibility for our own actions.

The terrible part about these eroded *gates* or *walls*, they can last for years, leaving deep emotional scars for years, leaving bottomless mental and emotional scars and problems in our lives, as well as the lives of others. As children of God, we lack the knowledge, like that of a parent in the natural sense. Likewise, our knowledge compare to God's superior knowledge is vastly limited. We simply will have to learn to build confidence and trust in God in the same manner as a child does its parents

However, when we do make bad mistakes, God is merciful and kind to give us restoration again. He will strengthen and bless us so that we can go through these dim moments of our lives, provided we repent for not consulting him in the first place. We then must pray for godly wisdom so that we will recognize and understand the difference. Through our experiences, we can one-day help someone else avoids the same pitfalls we have just come through.

The Gates of Hope

Hope deferred make the heartsick: but when the desire comes it is a tree of life. **Proverbs 13:12**

Hope can be defined as that indispensable link between success and failure, life and death. It is the last alternative before giving up entirely. In classical Greek literature, the word hope *(elpis)* refers to anxious thoughts about what is going to happen in the future. Depending on the situation at hand, it will determine the person's level of fear or joyful feeling.[2] Solomon said that when a person's hope is *deferred,* it means that their expectation of a good outcome has now *been postponed* or *delayed.* A good example of this is found in the book of Ezra and Nehemiah. Before Ezra and Nehemiah's arrival the Jews were in a state of hopelessness and had given up all interest in *restoring the gates* and *walls* of their city.

Yes, there were often times I would look at a bad situation in my own life and feel it was no use in trying to deal with it anymore. Naturally, at that point, *the gate of my hope* for any good outcome was then placed under attack by the tricks of the satan who sought to confuse and depress me. Failure to recognize the danger of such an attack only led me into a state of *hopelessness* and from that point to covering up my sense of hopelessness by first, running away from people, either mentally or physically, or, simply finding some sort of activities in which painful thoughts could be drowned out. Especially, when it made the heart very sick for duration of time. I simply drench facing squarely the problem. Finally realizing that retracting into a state of hopelessness only spelled defeat, I began to fast and pray. The Holy Spirit then revealed to me while in prayer that we are saved, that is, kept by the power of **our hope** (exceptions) in God. For behind every dark cloud the sun does shine whether we see it or not! (Roman 8:24,25).

24 For in this hope we were saved. But hope that is seen is no hope at all. Who hopes for what he already has? 25 But if we hope for what we do not yet have, we wait for it patiently. Romans 8:24-25 (NIV)

A wonderful feeling came over me as I realized the darkest part of the night only reveals that the sun is just over the horizon. I began to display, **I am going to win, I going to win,** attitude, which was all I needed to pull through. In addition, this new *winners* attitude was continually a stimulant and important link to patience as well. Note the last part of **Proverb 13:22**; but, when the desire comes; that is, my whole emotion and reactions then change. Like a tree drawing it's nutrient from a flowing nearby stream, so was my spirit and drive to move forward in God. How can you be sure of patience if your hope (expectations) has never been challenge? Thus, we must conclude, effectiveness of patience hinges upon the very fact that our level of hope in God and ourselves must be secure as well.

The gates/walls of Purpose

The New Thesaurus dictionary defines purposes as one intends to do, or achieve: one's aim or ambition, goals set or an objective. It also means an unsavory firmness of character. In fact, the opposite of the above definition is purposeless. This type of *purposeless* is a delightful tool of satan, which he made a common practice either confusing or torpedoing ones' spirit with confusion. Every move you make becomes senseless as well as the courses or routes to travel then being unclear. Peter in his writings to the church declares that we are not people without direction or purpose. In fact, he said:

> But ye are a chosen generation, a royal priesthood, a holy nation, and peculiar peoples.

The older saints use to have an old saying; this was not done in the hidden corner. When God selected us, it was divinely and openly done. He then made us an royal priesthood, that is, called to royal dominion or clothed with royal dignity. Then Peter goes on to say that though we be different ethical or cultural, may show forth together, the praises of him; (the glorious attributes of God), who hath called you, **(Gentiles, Jews, black or white;)**, out of darkness into his marvelous light (clear purpose for righteousness). (1 Peter 2:9) Author's emphasis:

Including with this chapter, we put forth these truths:

1. God wanted his people to be in a place of authority.

2. God not only desires that we as a people be restored, but that each of us should distributing the power with healing to others in need as well.

3. We have the right to show forth the glorious attributes of restoration that can only be found through Christ.

Chapter 9

Restorational Ministries

We do realize that this is a different era than of that in the Old Testament and that rebuilding the walls of people's lives requires a somewhat different approach. Nevertheless, the rules for achieving success on small or large scale in both the Old and New Testament never has changes; the workers under Nehemiah leadership and the New Testament church accomplished their goals using the *"Four rules"* of the thumb" which the believer today can successful follow to accomplish its own revivification effort as well.

1. Team effort
2. Trust and respect
3. Following the leader
4. Seek for the common goal

Along with these suggest rules, here are some vital questions that each member of the restorational team should ask themselves:

A. What can I do to make the teamwork efforts better and not worse?

B. Do I really trust and respect the gifts and talents of other people?

C. Am I willing to follow the leader's vision for providing restoration?.

D. What can I do more to promote the common cause of restoration to the entire body ministires

It is here that we seek to focus on the *fivefold ministries*, along with the *supporting gifts* provided in the church as the vital tools by which renewal is guarantee to its spiritual body.

Team player for Restoration

So God has appointed some in the church for his own use first, Apostles, second, prophets; third; teachers, then wonderworkers, then those with ability to heal the sick, helpers, administration, and speakers in different tongues. **Corinthians' 12:28 amplified Version. Note also, Ephesians 4:11;** *And he gave some, apostles; and some, prophets; and some, evangelists; and some, pastors and teachers.*

Paul, in both (1 Corinthian 12:28), and (Ephesians 4:11) scriptures gives us a clear picture of a spiritual team like that of a baseball team that has nine players; each play their own part. The team are guided by a manager who is responsible for the team's strategy to win and also its conduct. Nehemiah had twelve tribal families, and each tribe went along with excitement repairing the walls and gates in the surrounding areas where they lived. They completed the projects in sprite of the numerals problems with surrounding enemies, including, interesting, the Tekoites tribe's noblemen, who refuse to help out with the rebuilding effort. (Nehemiah 3:5). I will deal more with these noblemen later in the chapter. All of the gifts that God have provided as Paul explains in both scriptures are equally important and must operate in the same fashion as our human bodies operate, working in harmony with each other. Otherwise, the body being disfunction will suffer lack if serious attention is not given to compensate for the lost member, hense, serious problems.

Members within the body of Christ do become disfunctin sometimes, or may just lack clear understanding as to how their individual spiritual gifts should work within the framework of the church.

At a church where I formerly ministered in the early 80's, there were a few members that had lost the proper idea of what was their place in the body of Christ or in the local church where they attend. Their focus appear to had become distorted to the point that they did not really know where they were going. I had just started ministering at that church and was real curious and would ask a lay member: "What is your purpose or role in the ministry: would ask the class teacher/director: What are your short and long-range plans for this class or department? I also ask the minister(s) about their long or short range plans; in short, I wanted to know if everyone was certain of his or her roles. Some thought they knew, other responses from the lay leaders were confusing. A few of the brothers just rub their heads with puzzled looks on their faces before they could even enunciate an answer. These people mean well and were loyal to their church, but they had never really thought about or *clearly* understood how their gifts function in the body. No one ask them that kind of questions before, about goals, work plans, job description, etc. It was just business as usual. Or, should we say in some cases, bored business as usual.

I frequently find this attitude across the country with many churches and this kind of attitude may largely account for the failures in these people's services to God.

Trust and Respect

Below, is a illustration as how the *leading ministries* would picture in relationship with a human body (1 Corinthian 12:11-29).

The Apostles- *the head*

The Prophets - *the eyes*

The Teachers -*the legs*

The Pastors - *the hands*

The Evangelist- the feet

The rest of the ministries that are mention by Apostle Paul operates somewhat like *supporting agencies* to the *fivefold ministries.*

The gifts of Help

The gift of miracles, tongues, etc.

The gifts of administration

In (verse 27) Individually, we are like the nine players on the baseball team, yet, we are members together. Each member on the team must respect and trust the other person's ability and gift to operate distinctly. Just like the *head* must trust *the feet* to walk the rest of *the body* to the car, *the feet* must trust the *head* to give clear directions *to the body* so that *the feet* could carry the body where it suppose to go. Otherwise, if various parts of the body don't respect or trust the distinct ability of the others, you got a confuse and mis-functional operation. Imagining the head trying to do what the feet suppose to do; or, what about this, imagining the outfielder on the baseball team trying to do the pitcher's job. Who's going to catch the ball out in the outfielder's section?

(21) *That they may all be one. As you, Father, are in me and I am in you, may they also be in us, so that the world may believe that you have sent me. (22) The glory that you have given me I have given them, so that they may be one, as we are one,*

(23) *I abide in them, and you abide in me that they may become completely one with us, so that the world may know that you have sent me and have loved them even as you have loved me. (John 17:21-23) (NRSV)*

We should note here in this verse, that Christ desired that the body would *be one* as he and His Father are one. **(John 17:21,22).**

Following the leader

Nevertheless, as with every team, there must be a leader. Everybody cannot lead at the same time; that may be common knowledge, yet, leaders tend to have serious problems in this area. As stated earlier, the baseball manager is responsible for the team's strategy and conduct. It that true, than in order for the leader to be

confident of a winning team he or she would need to have three types of followers:
1. People who could follow directions.
2. People who willingly accept constructive criticism.
3. People who refuse to harbor selfish motives and agendas.

For a brief moment, go back and read (Nehemiah 3:5). Nehemiah receives cooperation from all the workers except for those important noblemen mention in verse 5. To put it plain and simple, the Tekoites noblemen, who was generally considered high ranking statesmen in their communities, did the exact opposite of the *rule.* They didn't trust or respect Nehemiah as the governor, or the team members efforts; they apparently had their own agendas, and goals.

It probably was a delight to Nehemiah's spirit to know that Tekoite's noblemen consist of only the faction of the population though they made have attempt to use their influence to disrupt the work on the wall. Otherwise, if theTekoites noblemen and anybody that like them were the majority they would wreck havoc in any project; yesterday, today and tomorrow. Unless God doesn't somehow use the 'stiff necks' behavior to further your causes to success then to hinder, the ability to restore lives may be drastically hindered.
Some of the suggest personality traits of these *noblemen* types people are mention here:
1. They seek to divide and conquer any good effort .
they say just enough to keep themselves conceal.

2. They would use whatever means available to them for personal gain.
3. They were liars, but knew how to *mix* truth in what
4. Their motives and agendas were usually spiritually dangerous to those seeking restoration for themselves and others.

The Common Goal

*(12) For the perfecting of the saints, for the work of the ministry, for the edifying of the body of Christ: (**Ephesians 4:11-12**).*

Like the Corinth Church that Paul preaches out, people that I know are seeking to popularize one office against another. This only creates jealousy and a lack of appreciation for the body ministries of that church. Believe me, it's sad. I personally know of ministers who have gone into pastoral ministry without a realistic call of God; because *I quote*: "Being a lay-minister or just an evangelist doesn't give me enough prestige." The bigger my name title is , the more important I feel that I am in the church. If the people under Nehemiah and Ezra had been fussing over role plays, they would have been destroyed for good. Obviously, anyone today, who makes such statements about their role play in the church don't value or appreciate their previous calling or role-play in Christ.

Now, because of a lack of understanding or appreciation, fulfilling the church's purpose for restoration in the body as Christ sees fit will now suffer and the **some** parts of the body ministry will be affected. Such disintegration of the team efforts causes the church to miss its goal while the enemy of our souls will gradually win. Every time there is a turnover or everyone has his or her own agenda in the church, satan scores while we unaware, will lose valuable opportunities to restore somebody's life that is in our hands.

Nevertheless, whatever our motives and objectives is in the ministry, our gift as it is use will still have its own degree, of progressive, weakness, and strength according to the level of our individually faith, services, and discipline we have in God's services. Howbeit, God will judge the manner by which each of us have facilitate our service when He returns.

Chapter 10

Re-Establishment

What to do
Nehemiah 4:1-23

Nehemiah mobilized his forces swiftly in an effort prevents the enemies from ruining their chances to be reestablish again. However, within a short time they encountered problems with Sanballet and Tobiah, two of the main adversities of the nation. Sanballet while having conferences with the Samaria army and his brethrens decides to lashes out at Nehemiah and the workers; assuming too, he was going to attack as well. Note his intimating words and ludicrous statement against the Jewish people.

Note the insulted question he asked.
1. What are these feeble Jews doing?
2. Will they restore things at will?
3. Will they try to bribe their God with

sacrifices?
4. Will they finish up in a day?
5. Will they revive the stones out of the heaps of rubbish, seeing they are burned?

Tobiah the Ammonite was near him, and said, what they build, if a fox climbs upon it, will break that weak stonewall down anyway. He and Tobiah though it was very preposterous for them to rebuild on weak walls; most of the walls were indeed charred.
Nehemiah 4:1-3

Sanballat felt that he knew the Jews were defeated by the plight of their long years of suffering, and even their integrity due to a broken fellowship with God Almighty. No doubt too, he had put together a team of *watchdogs* assign to watch Nehemiah and reporting the Jewish people well-being or whereabouts at all times. Could it have been those noblemen that refuse to put their neck to work as report in (Nehemiah 3:5)? At any rate, he was prepare at a minute notice to engage in public criticism of the nation for trivial matters, if they thought it would be beneficial to them. The workers on the wall were label, *"feeble Jews."* Which is to actual to say, how could this Jewish people re-establish the wall and gates if they hadn't done anything about in over seventy years; the walls themselves are burned badly.

Nehemiah 4:2,3
"Can they, through some ungodly, subtle manner, pull God into a phony deal to help them?"
Base on his past knowledge, he knew that was very unlikely as well. **The last question:** *"Can they finish restoring the gates/walls in one day?"*

Nehemiah prays for re-establishment
Nehemiah 4.4
Nehemiah prayed. Hear, O our God, for we are despised; turn their taunt upon their own heads, and give them up for prey in a land of their captivity.

Word was passed on to Nehemiah what Sanballat and his friends had said. Nehemiah then went back into his private prayer chambers and prayed that God would *"reverse"* the taunting upon his critics heads.
If one would look closer at this, even read the chapters along with this book, you will note that Nehemiah and the nation realize they didn't deserve the favor that was granted to them. I would be the first one to say, much of what good that has happen to me has happen to me as result of God throwing out all pending questions that was against me and through his mercy change the course of things for better in my life. Regardless how rightness any body thinks they are, we don't deserve the grace and mercy that comes our way. Thus, I have another chance each day I wake up to re-establishment of what I

lost in the past due to my own past brokenness.

Nehemiah 4:5

And cover not their iniquity. And let not their sin be blotted out from before thee: for they have provoked thee to anger before the builders.

I'm not too sure in *what manner* God would work that out today, but Nehemiah would. In fact, he would testify that aggressive behavior from others could help him move toward his blessing without them realizing it.

Nehemiah 4:6

So built we the wall; and all the wall was joined together together... for the people <u>had a mind</u> to work.

It was true that the gates had been in bad condition for over seventy years or more. But I believe Sanballet missed a very important point? He never knew about the impact of the revival that had taken place under Ezra and Nehemiah while they were there. This awesome revival made all the different for the people to have the proper mind to re-establish themselves as God had ordained. Including too, the hand of good favor from God was upon them. That brought all pending questions against them to a final closing. They had the right and clear signal from God through the Babylonia king to move ahead.

Expect opposition
Nehemiah 4:7-9

But when Sanballat, Tobiah, the Arabians, Ammonites and Ashdodites, heard that the walls of Jerusalem were going up, and that the breaches were being closed, they were very angry.

Any organized groups that oppose the righteousness of God can be placed in the category of foes. They are everywhere, in the church and at home. When these men heard that Jerusalem's breaches were being closed, they were angry. When your enemies see God removing the impossible in your lives and making things possible, your enemies will be walking around with rocks in their jaws, upset at what God is doing for you. In the Jews' case, the enemies should have been glad, but I can understand. If they really did not care about their national interests earlier, they certainly wouldn't be glad now.

Nevertheless, God will answer; and when He does, one or two of the following actions can be expected from him.

1. God will remove the problem(s) completely, or create a way to escape.

2. God will change our attitudes concerning the problem, so that we can become strong in the trial and finish the race.

3. God will use the foolish taunting of others to push us toward our goals.

They all plotted together to come and fight against

Jerusalem, to injure and cause confusion and failure. One gets the feeling that these perpetrators were quite an informed and trained group. They seemed to have had regular staff meetings. I am not sure if they knew Nehemiah's military strength, because if they did, they would have planned things a little differently. They probably felt confident that they had what it took to destroy the efforts of the Jewish people. I also honestly believe these conniving foes would sit up in the middle of the night, putting together plans for war games, just to undermine the strength of the Jewish nation's efforts. They may have started with ideological propaganda, that is, spreading bad rumors among the people. Wake up saints! Not only were the enemies ready to fight outside the walls, but they were also at an advantage, due to intermingling of the races.

The mere fact that some Jewish family's sons or daughters had married into the heathen nations made it rather easy for Sanballat and Tobiah to wipe out the Israelites. When it comes to making choices between your parents and a spouse, the spouse may become the loser in the pick. Which meant betraying? Satan knows this, and he is waging the same warfare in homes and churches now. He does not care about us becoming happy on Sunday mornings, just as long as he can keep you defeated during the week. When you get a chance, take a prayerful look around you. You will see spiritual war zones that wild spirits has set up in the church.

The Jewish nation's response (**vv. 6, 9**); but the people prevailed because they had a committed mind to finish the project. They made their prayer to our God, and set a watch against them day and night.

We are to be at peace with our enemies but also make known to God the things that are happening to us. The Spirit of God will then guide our hearts and minds through all the battles we fight.
(Phil. 4:5-7) **Author emphasis**.

The Problems more complex!
Nehemiah 4:10

The leaders of Judah said, The strength of the burden-bearers is weakening, and there is much rubbish; we have to move this mess out of the way before we can even put up new stones.

Below I have prepared an illustrational story that should show a analogous to the builders enormous pressure these wall builders may have been under. While reading this story remember this scripture:

Many are the afflictions of the righteous, but the Lord shall deliver them out of them all. (Psalm. 34:1)

Mary, now frightened of being hit again, moved cautiously away from the front door. She looked at her husband with what she knew was an inscrutable face. She felt very angry and betrayed. John quickly grabbed the door as if he could pull it off its hinges, swearing. Nervously, Mary asked, "Where are you going, John?" While staring at her John's eyes had the look of a mad man ready to blow up the house.

"I am going to have fun, and don't bother to look or call for me. I will come home when I get ready. Do you understand?"

Mary answered softly: she did. She remembered what happened before. Now this situation was happening again! Of course, she suspected where John's fun place is. She rushed into the kitchen and sat down at the kitchen table, crying softly to herself. "Lord, I do not know what to do about-- this kind of problem. It seems as if things are getting worst and worst." Mary had been in prayer two hours later when her phone rang. "Hi, this is Mr. Burton down at the police department." Police department? She wondered out loud.
"Yes, is this Mr. or Mrs. Mary Problems? "
"Yes it is, "she replies.
"We have a young man here, named Ricky Problems, is that your son? "
"Yes he is, what happen?"

"Well, your son is being locked up for procession of drugs. You can get him out with a bail payment for $3700.00 dollars."

The news suddenly hit Mary like a sledgehammer. "God, what is happening here?" Mary was beginning to feel like someone had thrust a knife into her heart. The pain was unbearable. There seemed to be more questions in her head now than were answers leaving her more and more confused. She quickly went into her bedroom and lay down. She prayed and cried. Prayed and cry; finally falling off to sleep.

Later that evening, Mary decided to go to the police station to pick up her son. Ricky standing against the wall rubbing his hands looked nervous. He never had been so embarrassed in his life. He was anxious to tell her about his new jail experiences and to explain to his mother that he was just in the wrong place at the wrong time and of course, she believes him. Yet, she knew all so well that her son still would have to prove his innocence in court later.

A week later, Mary's close friend called her up. "Mary, I got some bad news to share with you if you got a minute." Mary again braces herself.
"What the problem, Jenny?"
" Well, girl, you know that I wouldn't tell you nothing wrong. "

"I know I know Jenny. Mary, I heard that some big unfavorable problem is really boiling around the church. You know that you are a board member, in fact, I believe they've got you some how in the middle of it." Mary was trying to make some sense of what was happening on the phone when she heard footsteps. She turned around only to notice her 15 year old angry, confuse daughter, Laura, staring her in the face in the hallway with a small suitcase.

Laura was a stubborn person, and spoiled by her father. She felt that she was an independent person, and was always doing things her way despite Mary efforts to get her to conform.

She announced, "I'm leaving!"

"Where," mother asks her? "Don't know, in the streets maybe," the daughter answered coldly.

Mary looked at Laura look with surprise and unbelief. Apart from that, Mary knows that the government has taken her Biblical rights for disciplining her child (Proverb 22:15).

Folly is bound up in the heart of a boy, but the rod of discipline drives it far away. (Proverbs 22:15) (NRSV)

What am I going to do now, she wondered. Later that day, her husband called to say he thinking about leaving for good.

This is another illustration, enough to make any sane person buck and reel with anguish. Unlike this lady, you need not have done something wrong to merit these problems. There is a great chance that these angry demons are after your testimonies and the power God has placed in your life.

"Why attack my family or my finances?" you ask. That is a good question. Demons know the value of your integrity, your conviction, and your praise to God. He has studied your whole spiritual value system from day one you started your walk with Christ. He decides now that he will attack your things. Of course, while you are busy dealing with this shakeup, the devil figures you will take your mind off the most precious and valuable asset you have, that is, your praise to God. He will begin to weaken or take apart that "bridge of Praise" that always takes a saint across to God for sure victory. The enemy can and does take lots of things from us. However, we should never surrender our vision, our prayer life and praise to satan.

Satan's secret devilish attack
Nehemiah 4:11

And the enemies said, they will not know or see till we come into their midst and kill them and stop the work.

The enemy's plans to infiltrate and kill off the workers

are unknown. Probably too, the gates have been set up which would make it easy for them to come through at night and pierce a sword through the back of someone; Perhaps, they would disguise themselves in Jewish clothing. At any rate, it was shrewd and a crafty plans to disrupt the work. These evil spirits will develop situations that will lead to the same end.

(Ephesians 6:12); Paul says that we wrestle not against flesh and blood, but against principalities, against powers, and against the rulers of darkness of this world. Jesus declares their purpose in (John 10.9); so, thieves come to steal, kill and destroy.

These angry demons will stop at nothing until he has destroyed your will to fight. Then the devil will drag you down the road of guilt and despair, and finally, deteriorate your spiritual life in Christ.

Satan's game plan

For such are false apostles, deceitful workers, transforming themselves into the apostles of Christ? Don't be surprised, for Satan himself is transformed into an angel of light and will look quite innocence to most people. He knows how to blend in with normal church-folks. And, because of that blending strategy, his ministers can transform or change themselves into the ministers of righteousness without actually being righteous, whose ends shall be according to their works. (2 Corinthians 11:13-15). **Author emphases**

Fight for Re-establishment
Nehemiah 4:13-23

In these verses you will find Nehemiah putting together a wall repair and as well as a war strategy to keep the workers going. Nehemiah's motivation techniques were the greatest I have seen to date. He gives everybody their job description and places reinforcement wherever needed, scattering the group over the full length of the wall. No one fusses about who is more important at this point. Every person's part was vital to the security and success of the project.

Nehemiah says to them: "Fight for your families and loved ones." (Neh.4: 14)

While some were working, others had their swords in their hands ready at a minute notice to do battle if necessary. Naturally here, he was talking about spears and swords. Our type of warfare against the enemy is of different sources.

(2 Corinthians 10:4-5) The weapons of our warfare are not of the fleshly type. They are might through God, pulling down strongholds and casting down imaginations and every high thing that exalts itself against the knowledge of God. Bringing into captivity every high minded thought to the obedience of Christ.

Some of us can remember as an adolescent having quite a number of confrontations. And in reflecting back, we quickly recognize three battle mistakes we should have avoided against our opponents. However, these confrontations later lay the groundwork wherein we could learn to do war in the spiritual sense, especially as a born-again Christian.

1. <u>Never look down while fighting your opponent</u>. This indicates that we are not being alert or are remorseful about entering the fight in the first place. Worse still, the possibility of underrating our ability to fight effectively will surface.

2. <u>Never fight on slippery surfaces,</u> which merely becomes a problem with keeping your balance. You're sliding too much.

3. <u>Never fight in mud unless you have no choice!</u> The embarrassment of being covered with mud is unbelievable. The burden of this mud could render a person powerless. The whole ordeal will leave you emotionally impoverished and feeling humiliated and regretful.

Whenever I fought in a slippery or muddy area, I would simply stop fighting, turn around quickly and begin crawling out of the slippery or muddy spot before the other guy caught me and then regain my balance to fight again.

The Prophetic Way to Fight

The flip/flop prophetic side to this: You are not as prepared as you should be when you are looking down. In the Book of (Judges 7:5-7), Gideon sends 32,000 men home, simply because they were frightened, timid, or not alert.

In (Psalm 137), the Jewish people's sadness caused them to hang their "heads down," meaning a self-pitying feeling on its' grandest scale.

In (Psalm 27), we are encouraged to hold our heads up and wait on the Lord's deliverance. If God with is us, then who can be against us?

In continuing this lesson, *Slippery surfaces* can be any unsettled convictions or influence that tends to pull us in confusing directions. Paul warned us in (Ephesians 4:14) and (Hebrew 13:9) to stay away from every wind and doctrine that is not sound in scripture, thought, or purpose.

We must no longer be children, tossed to and fro and blown about by every wind of doctrine, by people's trickery, by their craftiness in deceitful scheming. (Ephesians 4:14) (NRSV)

Do not be carried away by all kinds of strange teachings; (Hebrew 13:9b) (NRSV)

129

Move away from the muddy surface if possible. Life does carry with it wounds, scares, friction, and hostile attitudes, along with abusive behavior. It's difficult enough to deal with parties that cover up this type of muddy situation, but more troubling is when you are being dragged into this same kind of conflict. That is, whatever you are receiving from them, you give back the same.

Looking down and wallowing in mud means depression and a defeated attitude. However, crawling out is any progressive plan or process used to retreat from the spirit of defeat. Finding dry ground is the power to move prayer along with the spirit of praise that will allow you to come with a strong grip on the situation at hand. When you are able to stand up and face your adversaries again, you can count on the Holy Spirit to assist you in receiving that spiritual breakthrough in your life.

It is here that God is giving you another chance to remove the rubbish of broken walls and burned down gates in your life and start rebuilding again. Maybe it's the wall of self-denial that needs restoring. If so, learn to accept the things you need. The things you honestly know that you do not need turn away. Examine the way you look at problems of a difficult nature, and don't look at them as something that is hard. Instead, look at them as if they are challenges, waiting for you to master. And when the patience is work out in us over a period of time, it then seems to develop within us a good, *sound experience. And that experience* has caused us to "know"

God more in the power of His might and grace.
We now have, good, confirmed hope in God. Because
of the soundness of that hope we are not ashamed, and
do not walk with our heads down defeated, because
God's unreachable love is being planted deeply every
day into the saints hearts by the Holy Ghost, which is
given to those who ask for it. He freely gives! (Roman
5:3-5) Author emphases

Chapter 11

A Consistent Winner
Nehemiah 6:1-17; 7:1

*Now when Sanballat, Tobiah, Geshem the Arab, and
the rest of our enemies heard that I had built the wall,
and there was no breach left in it, although at that
time I had not set up the doors in the gates.
Sanballat and Geshem sent to me, saying, Come, let
us meet together in one of the village in the plain of
Ono. But they intended to do me harm.*

Keep Your Place

Ono was near Lydda, in the plain country
bordering Philista. It was approximately 60 miles from
Jerusalem. You could add a few more miles to that from
the temple itself. The valley of Ono was a beautiful
sentry area that lies approximately five miles from the
Great Sea. But why would Sanballat and Geshem request
a meeting in that valley? I believe that Nehemiah was a
very hospitable person and would have set up a very

nice tent, equipped with soft pillows and lots of food right there in Jerusalem. Maybe the choir would have provided some soft holy music while Nehemiah and others discuss business or resolve problems.

In the first place, Ono was too far from Nehemiah's home base. Secondly, God had already provided Nehemiah with his important work and he need to move on and finish it. And even with a stallion racehorse along with a super chariot, it would have taken several hours to get to Ono. To me, this was another crafty plot by Sanballat to pull this important servant far from their post, wound Nehemiah and his band, leaving them in the plains to die. Most christians today would be grateful that Nehemiah had enough wisdom to know satan's devices and stay in his place instead.

It's possible that beliefs and practices, though they are traditional and well intended can still yet be dangerous if it is gradually pulling you too far from home base (Bible).

Some of the belief and practices we seen lately may well need to be looked at again to see if its lining up with the word of God. Again, some of the biblical doctrines that we declare are obsolete, trivial, or have no relevance to the church world today may very well be the principles we need to circumvent satan's devices and prevent being wounded and left dandling with little or no power to survive.

Be Consistent with the Word

There is nothing obsolete, trivial or irrelevant in the <u>Word of God </u>and it will offer refurbishment for the saints just like the Brook of Cherith offer relief for Elijah in 1 King 18:2-7.

Let's take Hebrew 12:14 for an example: "Follow peace with all men holiness without which no man shall see the Lord." (KJV)

This scripture may not be a favorite to everybody, however, if one would scholarly, *study* this verse and then *applied* its word to their lives in a practical and as well as a spiritual sense, they will come away with a much better health, save relationships, inner peace and tons of other restoratives.

Rather we do, or do not believe or understand this verse, it is just as powerful as those ravens that took care of Elijah. The problem is, once we move out of the word of God, and start moving into some other strange realm, you have lost your covering and without the mercies of God the contract that satan had on your life or possessions can be carry out to total destruction.

Careful evaluation of many Christians I know seem to exemplify behaviors like the soap opera actors on television, except the Christian brother or sister role is real. They are nervous and seem to live on the edge of each night that comes, waiting for a prophetic word from somebody. Many of us also found these same persons become despondent if they didn't receive a *word* or *cue* to move forward that they would lose all hope to wait for God to work things out for them. Sometimes, these same people will be tempted to find some 1-900-pychic reading company to help them find their answer instead of opening the Bible, believing the word for what is says.

The Bible is filled with all the cues and relevance's anyone will ever need! Including too, God has already placed genuine, anointed, and hardworking Bible preachers/teachers in your path to guide you through. However, you must remember that the Bible is a restorative meal laid out like a menu. When it is served to you, it is your hour to rise and eat, and please don't be ashamed. Be like a bulldog with meat in its mouth; refuse to turn the promise of the blessing loose until God has fulfilled his WORD in you.

Keep your Focus

Another problem is, that people sometime will become distracted from their "rebuilding efforts," both personally and in the lives of others. When you allow others to succeed in distracting you, they gradually are causing you to *"wandering away."* As Solomon says in the book of Probverbs 27:8

A bird that wandered from her nest- so is a man that wanders from his place.
David says we must maintain a desire to not wander

away from God's word. **Proverbs 27:8; Psalms 119:9-11**

Learn to use what you have

In all actuality, we must never cease to work hard to keep whatever, God has entrusted in our hands with all prayer and courage. Well, you may say, I don't have anything.

In **Matthew 25:14-30;** Careful reading of these scriptures will point out that God doesn't give every Christian the same amount or level of gifts, but He does give everybody the same chance to develop what they do have. The story ends on a sad note. The servant with the one talent just sat around complaining. Worse yet, he started to pity himself. In **verses 29** and **30;** the Lord took that which he didn't even have, and gave that talent to the man who already had much! My friend, take a friendly hint. Never, ever ask or look to God to give you more, if you never try using the talents God has already given you.

We should remember, God does not bless us according to our greatness in ability, but rather on our faithfulness to the *"little corner"* of our work that we do for him. I feel that will involve everything from street corner ministry to church ministries and everything that falls in between!

Stay on top of things

It is not a wise idea to make mistakes simply to learn from them because that can be very costly. However, if your decision doesn't turn out as you planned, never allow it to continue to be a stumbling block for you. Mistakes can, if you allow them, become a training tool. I encourage you to pray that, along with other valuable lessons, they'll make you better in some way in the future. At the same time, bad decisions that are made without proper consult with God should now teach us about our human inadequacies, too. This should also encourage us to listen more to those "still quiet voices" of God that speak to our hearts when we are alone, either at church or at home.

Never allow yourselves to live in the shadow of past mistakes. The contrast of handling things "on top" is when past mistakes nag you and you do not know how to release the guilty feelings from your mind. Thinking about those mistakes can be detrimental, when they are looked at in a negative manner. On the other hand, when you think of how things could have been done better, you will be able to help others avoid the same mistakes. More importantly, the past has turned into a positive experience.

Nehemiah 6: 5-7

Then Sanballat sent his servant to me again the fifth time with an open letter. **Nehemiah 6:5**

Sanballat and his allies' antipathy for Nehemiah drove

138

them still to another fruitless attempt to disturb the work on the walls/gates. This plan was by sending an official-type letterm arked "*open*" from a king (which according to custom was to be sealed). The letter and its contents being open as well would cause panic among the workers.

> *(Verse 6,7); in it was written, It is reported among the neighboring nations, and Gashmu says it, that you and the Jews plan to rebel; therefore you are building the wall, that you may be their king, is the report.*
> *Also you have set up prophets to announce concerning you in Jerusalem, There is a King in Judah. And now this will be reported to the {Persian} King. So, come now and let us take counsel together.*
> **Nehemiah 6:6, 7**

It is amazing how Sanballat put this one together. Nehemiah had placed his workers in their proper places and now the enemies see that. He then places his friend, Gehem Arabic neighbor, as a front-man to cover him from the public eye. I have been wondering how much money Gehem got out of that.

Nehemiah keeps the faith
Nehemiah 6:8

I replied to him, no such things as you say have been done; you are inventing them out of your out of your mind. For they all wanted to frighten us, thinking their hands will be so weak that the work will not be done. But now strengthen my hands!

Nehemiah seems to be in full charge. He puts forth no battle of words, but just a simple, straight-up response. Excellent speech doesn't fit or abide with a foolish person. Much less, lying lips with an official prince. Show a good life without being false. Holy speech that cannot be condemned by the world, so that they that are not born- again may eventually be ashamed by watching your life. By that account, their condemning will be reversed on them. When the enemies come against you like a flood, God will set up a high standard of your character before people! I believe Nehemiah must have reflected on this verse in the book of Proverbs.

Fine speech is not becoming to a fool; still less is false speech to a ruler. Prov 17:7 (NRSV)

Beware of deceptive strategies
Nehemiah 6: 10-13

I went into the house of Shemaiah, son of Delaiah, son of Mehetabel, who was shut up. He said, let us meet together in the house of God, within the temple, and let us shut the doors of the temple; for they are coming to kill you, at night they are coming to kill you.
But I said, should such a man as I flee? And what man such as I could go into the temple (where only the priests are allowed to go) and yet live?

I will not go in. And lo, I saw that God had not sent him, but he made this prophecy against me because Tobiah and Sanballat had hired him. He was hired that I should be made afraid and does as he said, and sin, that they might have matter for an evil report with which to taunt and reproach me. My God, think on Tobiah and Sanballat, according to their works, and on the prophetess Noadiah, and the rest of the prophets, who would have put me in fear.

Shemaiah, one of Jerusalem's prophets, apparently had an apartment adjoining the Temple. The reason Nehemiah went there is not known. He may have been given an urgent message from this prophet to come. When Nehemiah does arrive, the prophet is putting together some false story about a contract being on Nehemiah's life. He quickly suggested that they should shut themselves up in the place of Holy of Holiness. Nobody in Jerusalem beside the high priest would want to go in there. It was a strict violation of Jewish law. Nehemiah simply refused that offers, and never enter into a war of words with the prophet. He was firm with this false prophet, yet tactful with his wording. (Verse 11); Nehemiah had discerned the prophet's spirit and intent. (Verse 12), Nevertheless, he never allowed the prophet to know what God had revealed to him concerning the payoff.

David declared: Though a host should encamp against me, my heart shall not fear; though war should rise against me, in this will I be confident. **Psalm 27:3,4**

The project is finish!
Nehemiah 6:15, 7:1

So the wall was finished the twenty-five day! in the month of Elul (Aug-Sept), in fifty-two days! Now it came to pass, when the wall was built, and I set up the doors, and the porters and the singers and the Levities were appointed. Nehemiah 6:15

According to history reports, the walls around Jerusalem were probably finished in the month of September in a record fifty-two days! Contrary to some arguments, we believe the story is true and not a fiction at all as much of the walls surrounding the old city in Jerusalem today are believe to be laid by the hands of Nehemiah and his workers. Remarkably, the walls have stood as a monument for 4000 years or more as a reminder of the great skill and faith of these Jewish people. I believe you too, are convinced that Nehemiah was indeed an organized man with a vision and a purpose and showed great skill in thwarting enemy attacks and motivating people to work! Jesus declared in (Luke 14:28-30) that a person is not wise when they don't make proper preparation for any project.

Prophetic, it means that all of us as born-again believers has only a limited time to rebuild our nation. Thank God for those who have already redeem some of that limited time while sharing the gospel of Jesus Christ. Nevertheless, satan recognizes what you are doing and the limited time as well, and is seeking to sabotage the quest for restoration in all of our lives.

The new challenge before us

In this final summary, Christian's workers of all levels are challenged to strive even harder in restoring or repairing the breaches in other people now. Nehemiah took the challenge willingly. However, he clearly unfolded the vision before actual work began on the walls and gates according to (Nehemiah 2:11-16). These people quickly saw the sincerity of their leader, however, success of that building occurred *only* when the people responded in obedience to directions that Nehemiah and his official staff gave. Nehemiah gave all their job descriptions. None would overlap with another worker, but each carried out their jobs with a spirit of joy and faith.

Lay-members sometimes doubt the outcome of projects simply because they cannot clearly see what or how God is revealing things to the leader. I'm sure God will not give ten people the same vision. Nevertheless, I do believe He will confirm the vision with the ten and show them how to HELP carry the leaders' vision out. But God only deals with one leader at a time, whether it's the whole church or local departments in the church. The rest follows. It is also true too, that we will not know how God will work things out. We just know as Brother Shambach, a well-known speaker, often says, "THAT GOD DOES IT AND WHEN HE DOES IT, HE DOES IT WELL!"

Possessing the Gates

The above phrase *"possessing the gates"* simply means taking charge of your home, your ministries and your lives. The writer have tried to deal with the historical end, and yet give you the prophetic picture in hopes that the church today would see with a spiritual eye the profound way that Ezra and Nehemiah had dealt with the Jewish nation during its reforming period.

Its' not over yet!

It was Nehemiah desire that the Levites, priests and workers would know and feel secure in their boundaries and to recognize that the gates, walls were indeed vital to their protection. It also represents their covenant *title deed* of ownership as promise by God to Abraham. He taught the local leaders how to provide restoration in a meteor of unparalleled way, and use the people he had to steer the nation back to a greater victory and splendor. Nevertheless, this *restoration* stood only as a *shadow* to an even greater splendor still unknown to the chosen people. **It's not over yet!**

The question is: Through whom will such events come, and, by what fashion will it be completed? Included with this question was Israel's continual *up* and *down* spiritual cycles which only proved a need for a major reconciliation plan. The Messiah, as the **Lamb of God** would be the *connecting thread* through which the Jews and the world can be brought back to harmony and peace with God.

*Without the shedding of **his blood**, there cannot be any remission from sin. **Hebrew 9:22.***

Today, the Christian world faces the continual challenges of making known to the world such reconciliation opportunities, which provide *restoration*. Without it, the nations' capital and the world stand to crumble under the load of its crisis. Naturally, we do not have to go very far. There are emotional damaged walls right in our backyards, neighborhoods and cities. Therefore, the need for *restoration* in many lives continues to go on.

PART 4

The
Thousand
Year
Millennium Rule

Chapter 12

The Final Countdown!

The first advent of the nation of Israel's restoration, and their being the channel of salvation for the Gentile world, has been the focus up to this point. The prophets, by far, that deal with Christ's first coming also speak of His second coming with equal clarity. [1] The disciples ask Jesus a question:

Lord, wilt thou at this time restore again the kingdom to Israel? (Acts 1:6)

If you would note the question, it strongly pictured conditions in Judah at a time when the disciples were tired and frustrated of been politically oppress. They longed for a promised restoration that would bring about prosperity, honor and political power of which they had lost. They were dead serious about change and may have pondered on the many prophecies that had already gone forth concerning their state. Perhaps, this scripture could have been one of them?

(8) As for you, O watchtower of the flock, O stronghold of the Daughter of Zion, the former dominion will be restored to you; kingship will come to the Daughter of Jerusalem."
(Micah 4:8) (NIV)

Nevertheless, these faithful followers of Christ envisioned of material prosperity and political power was correct, but the timing was yet future. Jesus' momentary answer to them discourages the men from speculation about the Roman power, which rule them then...

(7) He said to them: "It is not for you to know the times or dates the Father has set by his own authority. Acts 1:7 (NIV)

Christ did not deny that there would not be a restoring of the kingdom back to the Jews, in fact, he only indicate that no one knows the year, month, week, day or hour that God Almighty decides to bring these things to past. Jesus then shifts their focus toward more important manners at hand then. [2]
Jerusalem was destroyed by Titus in 70 A.D. yet John in The Book of Revelations, written about 96 A.D. 26 years later, speaks of the Second Coming as still future. **Rev. 22:12,20** (3) the prophets foresaw the first exile and also Jerusalem being trodden down by the Gentiles until the

times of the Gentiles are fulfilled. [3] Nevertheless, they also prophesied that God would restore His people to their own land.

Know therefore and understand that from the going forth of the commandment to restore and to rebuild Jerusalem until the coming of the anointed one, (Christ), a prince, shall be seven weeks [of years], and sixty-two weeks [years]. It shall be built again with City Square and moat, but in trouble times.
Daniel 9:25

Nevertheless, as God's covenant people, the stage is rapidly being set for the Second Advent that will proceed with the tribulation period. These prophetic events of the Messiah's coming and Israel's final restoration is so abundant and comprehensive that it can be dealt with only in outline form. [4]

Jerusalem is located on a ridge of rolling hills 2,000 feet high in the western highlands of Judea. Historically, it is known as the land of milk and honey. Several prominent hills or mounts are frequently mentioned in connection with this city. The eastern hill of the city is Mt. Moriah, where some believe Abraham offered up his son Isaac as a sacrifice. Mount Olivet, with an elevation of 3000 feet high, is most frequently mentioned in the Bible lies directly east of the temple area. The Garden of Gethsemane is located on the lower

149

part of the western slope of the Kidron Valley. Samaria lies just north of Judea. Palestine, famous for its plains is the largest of the plains in Esdraelon. Many great events occurred there. Palestine lies between southern Galilee and northern Samaria and between the Mediterranean Sea and the Jordan Valley. Many famous battles were fought here since Biblical times. [5] Of course, this beautiful country has been ruled by more than a dozen foreign and local powers over its 4000 years history before its succeeded in gaining self-dependent and rule in 1948. During its long history it has suffered like no other nation through degradation, humiliation, oppression, and mutilation. Naturally, part of this suffering is due to their disobedience to God.

No peace within its walls!

On May 15, 1948, the official date for the end of the thirty-year British Mandate over Palestine, the Jewish provisional government proclaimed the independent state of Israel. The Jews, in opening the road to the old city of Jerusalem, immediately met Arab Legionaries attacking from every direction. With powerful modern war weapons, the enemies took the Jewish quarters in the old walled city of Jerusalem, which includes Mount Moriah. The Jews, suffering tremendous bombardment from Arab forces, were able to open a new road to the coastal plain, and food and ammunition again began to flow to the city. This new Israel fought with courage and spirit. Since its independence it has seen six wars within its walls. The 1948 War of Independence, the 1956 Sinai campaign, the Six-Day War of 1967, the War of Attrition with Egypt in 1969-71, the Yom Kippur War of 1973, and the Lebanon War of 1982. Over 15,000 Israeli deaths have scarred the landscape of this ancient land. Yet, it has managed to survive being ribbed apart.[6]

Today, this country stands divided between the Arab-Israeli's and Palestine's with the continual dispute relating to territory along the West Bank, the Gaza Strip, and the Golan Heights. Though many of the national and local peace keeping-groups have been working to reconcile the parties, the problems remain, with different ideologues deep and very complex. Armed attacks and cultural disharmony continues. And, many of the Arab-Jewish tensions are non religious, following the patterns of stereotyping, fear, envy, and wary friendships that are common to the prejudices between classes and ethical groupings elsewhere, like in America and South Africa. In fact, within Jerusalem's own walls there are diverse groups of small communities of Jews, Christians, Muslims, Roman Catholics, and Greeks, each zealously defeating their traditions and their faiths. Sometimes, as noted among the Arab Jews will kill each other in the name of God.

Creating a Conflict free environment?

There was an article in the *Israel Opposing Viewpoint* which point with admired an organization; named *The Zionist Format* in created an idea community. The idea community consists of democracy-political, social, and cultural-for the inhabitants of Israel, irrespective of religions belief, race or sex. However, with interest I questioned any of it could become reality until after the tribulation period. Human relationships between ethnic groups are already at a boiling point. *A New York Times article* read something like this:

Peace Center opens in Tel Aviv

Scores of foreign statesmen and business leaders showed up for Middle East peace moves today at the inauguration of a new peace institute founded by the Israelis Nobel Peace laureate Shmon Peres.

"Apparently we struck the right chord," said Mr. Peres, who is the architect the of Israelis historic Oslo Accord with the Palestinians. Mr. Netanyahu defeated Mr. Peres, a former Labor Party Prime Minister, in 1996.

The Peres Center for Peace is a private institute set up to promote peace through projects that foster economic opportunity. Mr. Peres said: "If we wait the cost of peace will not go down but if we wait the price of having peace will go up. None of us need a sixth Middle East war."[7]

The above concepts are good and I congratulate the

efforts of Mr. Peres along with others who try to promote such general ideas. But as long as satan rules, the evil strongholds that grip this land will never permit such harmony and peace among its citizens. An article from a *New York Time paper*:

Palestinians/Israeli conflict:

Doubts of peace seem to lie with Prime Minister Benjamin Netanyahu, who the writer considered to be an ambiguous figure, projecting no persuasive vision of a peaceful future. His focus is on satisfying the coalition that keeps him in power, many of whose members oppose any imaginable agreement with Palestinians. The finger of blame had been pointed at Yasir Arafat for the suicide bombing in Jerusalem, and for not preventing terrorism. There is plenty wrong with Yasir Arafat as a political leader. His regime is corrupt and brutal, as many Palestinians say. Prime Minister Benjamin Netanyahu crack down on the Palestinians aroused feelings of humiliation, resentment and hopelessness, reported Douglas Jehl of the *Times*. American diplomats know that the real difficulty in the peace process lies in the complexities of Israeli politics. What hope is there for progress toward peace in these circumstances?

There appear to be no realistic answers. [8] *New York Times paper: Palestinians/Israeli conflict 10\97.* Just recently, the *New York Times* reported in the Gaza, Israeli security

153

forces at a roadblock fatally shot a Palestinian.

In March 26\97: In Bethlehem, Hebron and Ramallah, Palestinian demonstrators and Israeli security forces clashed. Some 24 Palestinians were reported wounded.

In March\97 In Nablus, Palestinian security forces held back thousands of Palestinian demonstrators attempting to march on an Israelite post at Joseph's Tomb. Israeli tanks were deployed near the town in anticipation of violence. [9]

Christ's commandments rejected

Personally, these conflicts could have been minimized with the advice of Jesus:

Matthew 5:43; Ye have heard that it hath been said; Thou shall love thy neighbor, and hate your enemy.

Verse 44 But I say unto you, Love your enemies, bless them that curse you, do good to them that hate you, and pray for them which despitefully use you, and persecute you.

Most Jews in Jesus' time and even today would reject such teaching, but the principals would encourage peace and harmony within any community, and would be the best method in destroying conflicts. Instead, Jewish, Christians, Muslims, Roman Catholics, and Greeks each fight to zealously defeat their traditions and faith instead of Christ's teaching. These traditional concerns have done more to erode relationships then to enhance.

I personally encourge all parties the following advice:

*Wisdom generally will suggect, that quarreling people must find a **concrete, but <u>prudent reason</u>** to fin its anger at each other, or consider putting out its flame.*

To put it simply again: The above commandment from Jesus could have resolved generations of conflict between races in that region.

Jesus said, (verse **46**);

For if you love them, which love you, what reward have you? Do not even the publicans the same? *(Matthew 6:46)*

The culture tends along the West Bank, the Gaza Strip and Golan Heights only encourages each group to love its own. We understand that conflicts are deep and complex in that region. But whenever there is an attempt to cross over in reaching out beyond the borders to unite, that group or person will receive harsh criticism from their own. Perhaps the advice from Dr. Martin Luther King Jr. would be of some help:

"Now, let me suggest first, that if we are to have peace on earth, our loyalties must become ecumenical rather than sectional. Our loyalties must transcend our race, our tribe, our class, and our nation; and this means we must develop a

155

world perspective." [10]

The world watches with nervously, and interest with the prevailing question. Which ethnic group will win its fight for survival? Especially those who reside in the Gaza strip area where most of the conflict has been for the last thirty-five years. I believe those people around the world as well as in the Gaza strip who confess Christ, as Lord of their lives, despite their race, tribe, or class will eventually win in the fight for survival.

Chapter 13
The Redeemer is Coming!

Acts 1.11; reads, "This same Jesus, which is taken up from you into heaven, shall so come in like manner as ye have seen Him go into heaven.

15 For this we declare to you by the word of the Lord, that we who are alive, who are left until the coming of the Lord, will by no means precede those who have died.

16 For the Lord himself, with a cry of command, with the archangel's call and with the sound of God's trumpet, will descend from heaven, and the dead in Christ will rise first.

17 Then we who are alive, who are left, will be caught up in the clouds together with them to meet the Lord in the air; and so we will be with the Lord forever.   1 Thess 4:15-17 (NRSV)

This appearance of Christ is called the Rapture which he will suddenly appear to His own and take them away. All shall see Second Coming of Christ. **Hebrews 9:28; Revelation 1:7; Matthew 24:26,27.**

29 "Immediately after the distress of those days
"'the sun will be darkened, and the moon will not give its light; the stars will fall from the sky, and the heavenly bodies will be shaken.'
30 "At that time the sign of the Son of Man will appear in the sky, and all the nations of the earth will mourn. They will see the Son of Man coming on the clouds of the sky, with power and great glory.
31 And he will send his angels with a loud trumpet call, and they will gather his elect from the four winds, from one end of the heavens to the other.
  Matt 24:29-31 (NIV)
28 So Christ was sacrificed once to take away the sins of many people; and he will appear a second time, not to bear sin, but to bring salvation to those who are waiting for him. Heb 9:28 (NIV)
7 Look, he is coming with the clouds, and every eye will see him, even those who pierced him.
  Rev 1:7b (NIV)

Immediately after the *rapture* there comes a period of *false peace* set up by the Anti -Christ. Not long after that it will also include Christ sealing **His** special *messengers.*

> *And the king shall do according as he pleases...*
> *Neither shall he **regard** any gods, but will magnify*
> *himself above **the God** of gods... Thus he will prosper*
> *until his time is finished. And he will show no*
> *regards for any other god; he will **magnify** him above*
> *every god. But in his estate shall he honor the God of*
> *forces. Thus shall he do in the most strongholds with*
> *a strange god, whom he shall acknowledge and*
> *increase with glory: and he **shall cause them** to rule*
> *over many...* **Daniel 11:36-39**

Then I saw another beast(cruel ruler) rising up out of the land itself; he had two horns like a lamb and he roared like a dragon...he exerts all the power and right of control of the former beast in his presence, and causes the earth and those who dwell upon it **to exalt** and deify the first beast, whose deadly wound was healed,(relived again). And worship him. He performed **great signs**...startling miracles...even making fire fall from the sky to the earth in men's sight.

He **deceives** those who inhabit the earth, commanding them to erect a statue in the likeness of the beast that was wounded by the sword and still survived... He demands everyone, both small and great, both the rich and the poor, receive the mark or inscription of the name of the beast in their foreheads or hand.
No one had the **power** to buy or sell unless they had **the**

mark of the beast on him or her. **Revelation 13:11-17**

The Anti-Christ will succeed in a *temporary* one world government for three and one half years **2 Thessalonians 2: 1-12**. The groundwork for this operation *has already* being set. And to accomplish its insidious and perverse objectives, the leaders have *connected* into a common cause and agenda. This is done through any political social, educational, and religion organizations that support their agendas. The power of witchcraft and demonical spirits of satan strengthen this entire operation. But, the Holy One shall prune this land and earth of such ungodly influences.

It is the tragedy period for many who were not prepare for the *rapture*, and must now face the wrath of the Anti-Christ and its forces. These cruel people will quickly seek to destroy around the world any who profess the name of Jesus very much like the Babylonian soldiers mentioned in the **Second Chapter.** They killed with a smile on their face.

Satan declares war

So then the dragon (satan himself) was furious at the woman,(Jewish believers), and he went away to wage war on the remainder of Israel's descendants, who obey God's commandments and who have the testimony of Jesus Christ-and adhere to it and bear witness to Him. Revelation 13.17

To *this day* there is a special remnant of Jews, perhaps

scattered now, but will be there in Jerusalem or Palestine to hold up the name of Jesus in the earth.

Or do you not know what the Scripture says in the passage about Elijah, how he pleads against Israel?

*"**Lord**, they have killed Thy Prophets, they have torn down thine altars, and I alone am left, and they are seeking my life." But what is the **divine** response to him? "I have **kept** for myself seven thousand men who have **not bowed** the knee to Baal"* **Romans 11:2-2**

Gathering the special messengers

After this, I John, saw in the vision, four angels stationed at the four corners of the earth, firmly holding back the winds of the north, south, east and west from hurting the earth until ordered. There was complete calm.

Then I saw again a second angel coming up from the east direction, carrying the seal of the living God. And, with a loud voice, the angel who had been given authority and power earlier said to the four angels.

"Do not harm the earth or the sea or the trees, until we have sealed the one hundred and forty-four thousand bond-servants of our God on their foreheads." These are the special men who will be sealed.

*The of tribe of **Judah**, twelve thousand*
*The of tribe of **Reuben**, twelve thousand*

*The of tribe of **Gad**, twelve thousand*
*The of tribe of **Asher**, twelve thousand*
*The of tribe of **Naphtali**, twelve thousand*
*The of tribe of **Manesseh**, twelve thousand*
*The of tribe of **Simeon**, twelve thousand*
*The of tribe of **Levi**, twelve thousand*
*The of tribe of **Issachar**, twelve thousand*
*The of tribe of **Joseph**, twelve thousand*
*The of tribe of **Benjamin**, twelve thousand*
*The Lamb of God and the one hundred and forty-four
thousand* shall descend on Mount Olives: **(Rev.
7:1-8)**

They are the *one hundred* and *forty-four thousand
missionaries* that will go throughout the world carrying
the *gospel* of Jesus Christ during the latter part of the three-
and half-year. Just before the earth is shaken with great
catastrophes accompanied by earthquake, pestilence,
fire and mutual slaughter.

*And I, John, looked, and I saw the Lamb of God, (Jesus
Christ) along with the one-hundred and forty-four
thousand seal-bond servants standing atop Mount
Olives.*
*And I heard a voice from heaven. It was loud, like an
ocean, yet, it sound like a sweet melody of a harpist
playing their harps.*
*They sang a new song before the throne of God, and
before the four living creatures; along with the twenty-
four elders; no one on earth could interrupt or
understand the song but the one-hundred and forty-
four thousand seal-bond servants. They were pure men,*

162

undefiled before God's as special chosen messenger to the earth. **Revelation 14;1-5. emphasis placed.**

Get ready for the purging

And there came one of the seven angels which had the seven vials, and talked with me, saying unto me, Come hither; I will show unto you **the judgment** of the great whore that sits upon many waters:

With whom the kings of the earth have committed fornication, and the inhabitants of the earth have been made drunk with the wine of her fornication. When the one hundred and forty-four thousand is finished with their mission, then shall the *seven bowls* be pouring out on the earth? It is the beginning of the mass destruction of the earth called the time of Jacob's trouble. **24:15,29; and Revelation 3:10; 7:14.** This is the second part of the seven-year tribulation.

This tribulation will be worldwide, but the most intense trial will be in Jerusalem and Judea. It will be a period of suffering unsurpassed, " such as was not since there was a nation, no, nor shall be." **Daniel 12:1.** It will be far worse then Israel's Holocaust in 586 B.C. as mentioned in Chapter Four.

However, Isaiah explained the purpose of the event:
"To punish the host of **high ones** *that are on high, and* **the kings** *of the earth that are on the earth.* **Isaiah 24:21.**

The different in this tribulation is that *only* the enemies of the Lord God will suffer. However, Jesus did say that accept those days be shorten no flesh would be save... **Mark 13:20).**

John described the *last* World power:

> *I saw a woman sit upon a scarlet colored beast, **full of names** of blasphemy, having seven heads and ten horns.*
>
> *And the **woman was arrayed** in purple and scarlet color, and decked with gold and precious stones and pearls, having a golden cup in her hand full of abominations and filthiness of her fornication:*
>
> *And upon **her forehead** was a name written:*

**Mystery Babylon
the Great,
The Mother of Prostitues and
ABOMINATIONS of the earth**

And there are **seven kings**: five are fallen, and one is, and the other is not yet come; and when he cometh, he must continue a short space.

And the **ten horns, which thou saw,** are **ten kings**, which have received no kingdom as yet; but receive power as kings one hour with the beast.

These have one mind, and shall give their power and strength unto the beast.

These **shall make war** with the Lamb, and the

Lamb **shall overcome** them: for he is **Lord of lords**, and **King of kings**: and they that are with him are called, and **chosen,** and **faithful.**

And he said unto me, the **waters,** which thou saw, where the whore sits, **are peoples,** and **multitudes,** and **nations,** and tongues. And the **ten horns,** which thou saw upon the beast, these shall hate the whore, and shall, **make her desolate** and **naked,** and shall eat her flesh, and burn her with fire. And **the woman,** which thou saw, is **that great city,** which reigns over the kings of the earth. **Revelation 17:1-18.**

Following this, *"the chosen people"* will witness the wrath of God on their "long time" enemies, which will result in the final liberation of Israel. They are now called out from among the "curse."

*I then heard another voice from heaven saying, **come out** from Babylon, my people, so that you **may not share** in her sins, neither participate in her plagues. **Isaiah 48:20; Jeremiah 50.8.***

For Babylon's iniquities— crimes and transgression-are piled up as high as heaven, and **God has remembered** her wickedness. And the rulers and leaders of the earth, who joined Babylon in her immorality and idolatry and luxuriated will **weep** and beat their breasts **and lament** over her when they see the smoke of her conflagration **Ezekiel 26.16,17;**

165

Revelation 18.4,9 author's emphasis made. Christ, along with His accompanying saints and holy angels will now prepare to establish the long-promised Messianic kingdom in the earth.

"Pouring out!"

*(10) "And I will **pour upon** the house of David, and upon the inhabitants of Jerusalem, the <u>spirit</u> of grace and of supplications:*

*And they shall **look upon me** whom they have pierced, and they **shall mourn for him**, as one mourned for his only son, and shall **be in bitterness for him**, as one that is in bitterness for his firstborn."*

Zechariah 12:10; Jeremiah 31: 8,9

The phrase *"pour out"* is used literally to denote pouring something out of a vessel, such as water, etc. Here, it may refer to a physical or emotional revival of a person's spirit, such as the Jewish people pouring out of themselves genuine repentance toward Christ. [1]

God, Almighty will pour out of Himself to the remnant a different spirit of which the nation Israel never had before. A revived, yearning spirit. A spirit, which produced change of attitudes and positions, held earlier.

The house of David and Jerusalem will depict the kind of supplication and the sorrow that will follow the realization that they are guilty of killing the Messiah. They will wail and cry, perhaps, make their own "wailing wall" within the confines of their dwelling places.

Those who seek Me, I will show my favor toward them to seek Me even more. Who is a God like You that forgives our iniquity and have mercy on the transgression of the remnant (those that are scattered) of His heritage?

God will not retain His anger forever; because He delight I mercy and loving-kindness. God will again have compassion on us (Jews). He will vanquish and tramp out our iniquities. God will cast all of our sins into the depths of the sea. **Micah 7:18-19**

David says: As far as the east is from the west, so far has God removed our transgressions from us. **Psalm 103:12.**

House of David and Jerusalem

The term "David House" obviously didn't mean a building of stone and cedar. This term is often used to mean a family lineage, especially one of royalty. **Webster's Third New International Dictionary** gives a definition of house in this sense, "A family of ancestors, descendants, and kindred; a race of a person from the same stock, especially noble family."[2]

Hebrews 3:2 In this passage house is used to describe Israel collectively as God's special, chosen people. Here Paul explains in detail about **God's elected:**

Behold therefore the goodness and severity of God: on them (the Jews) which fell, as resulted of its own self-righteousness and rejecting the Messiah.

severity; but toward thee, as a Gentile believer, you still receives goodness.

If thou would continue in God's goodness you would be bless. Otherwise thou also shall be cut off. You and any unbelieving Jews would be eternal lost as well.

"If they abide not still in unbelief, shall be grafted in: for God is able to graft them in again." God may give the Jewish unbeliever another chance.

For if thou were cut out of the olive tree which is wild by nature, and were grafted contrary to nature into a good olive tree: how much more shall these, (Jews) which be the natural branches (elected people), be grafted into their own olive tree?

It is important that you should be not ignorant of this mystery, lest you should be wise in your own conceits; that blindness in has happened to Israel, until the fullness of the Gentiles be come in. But, after the tribulation, all Israel shall be saved: as it is written.

There shall come out of Zion the Deliverer (Christ), and shall turn away ungodliness from Jacob:(God shall provide cleaning and restoration for the whole nation of Israel). For this is my covenant unto them, when I shall take away their sins.

As concerning the gospel, they are enemies for your sakes now: As far as your acceptances of the gospel concerning Jesus Christ, they without knowledge hate you.

Nevertheless, as touching the election, they are beloved for the fathers' sakes. Yet, according to my covenant, they are my chosen people.
For they were begotten, or born of my Father by the spirit through Abraham, the father of faith. For the gifts and calling of God on us are without repentance. **Roman 12:22-29** author's emphasis made:

Look upon me:
(whom they rejected) **Zechariah 12:10**
The Prophet Zechariah here in the verse explained that Israelites would finally regret sorrowfully that they had not accepted or obey Christ's commandants as the most important remedy their restoration.

A fountain is available
*In that day there shall be **a fountain opened** to the house of David and to the inhabitants of Jerusalem for **sin** and for **uncleanness**.*
*And it shall come to pass in that day, said the LORD of hosts, that I will cut off the names of **the idols** out of the land, and they shall no more be remembered: and also I will cause **the prophets** and the **unclean spirit** to pass out of the land. **Zechariah 13:1**.*

The word fountain derives from the Latin *fons*, meaning, "source." These fountains may be described as the flowing have pressurized water up and out through an aperture from some hidden depth below the earth's surfaces.

The Jewish people understood this prophecy of Ezekiel, for there were folklore stories of remarkable springs and fountains in their time. The prophet Ezekiel's vision of Yahweh's *regenerated* Temple, a spring flows out from under the Temple. Its water caused perpetually bearing fruit trees to spring up at once along its banks.
This water demonstrates two additional potentialities attributed to certain sacred fountains, namely, healing and fruitful powers. [3]

In light of Ezekiel visions, God also can *create* and will create within the *souls of humanity* a *fountain* through which the cry for mercy and repentance will flow. It will come from the depth of God's wisdom and creativity, which is beyond humanity understanding.
The mere fact that He is Omnipotent, Omniscient, Omnipresent and Eternal gives Him the power to incorporate such blessings where needed.

Ezekiel explains Israel's sin and uncleanness"
Moreover the word of the LORD came unto me, saying, Son of man, when the house of Israel dwelt in their own land, they **defiled it by their own**

way and by their doings: their way was before me as the uncleanness of a removed woman.

Wherefore I **poured my fury** upon them for the blood that they had shed upon the land, and for **their idols** wherewith they had polluted it: **Ezekiel 36:16-20;**

I will cause the prophets and the unclean spirit to pass out of the land. **Zechariah 13,**

False prophets and unclean spirits are reinforced with television, movies, computer networks, and an array of high-tech media possibilities. This global evil will one day be cleared out completely.

Retiring the war machines

They shall beat their swords into **plowshares** and their **spears** into **pruning hook**: nation shall not lift up a sword against nation. Neither shall they learn war any more. **Micah 4:3; Isaiah 2:4;**

The explosive substances inside those missiles will doubly intensify earthquakes and further damages to warheads and planes to mere charred or burned pieces. And, if there be any worthwhile metal pieces left they would probably be used for farming purposes. In other words, Christ will *officially retire* all war machines when He returns.

Chapter 14

Celebration!

ll Samuel 7:12-17

The scriptures below will bare proof of the one thousand year Millennium rule that God promise to David.

12 When your days are fulfilled and you lie down with your ancestors, I will raise your offspring after you, who shall come forth from your body, and I will establish his kingdom.
13 He shall build a house for my name, and I will establish the throne of his kingdom forever.
14 I will be a father to him, and he shall be a son to me. When he commits iniquity, I will punish him with a rod such as mortal's use, with blows inflicted by human beings.
15 But I will not take my steadfast love from him, as I took it from Saul, whom I put away from before you.
16 Your house and your kingdom shall be made

sure forever before me; your throne shall be established forever.

In accordance with all these words and with all this vision, Nathan spoke to David. 2 Sam 7:8-17 (NRSV)
4 *I saw thrones on which were seated those who had been given authority to judge. And I saw the souls of those who had been beheaded because of their testimony for Jesus and because of the word of God. They had not worshiped the beast or his image and had not received his mark on their foreheads or their hands. They came to life and reigned with Christ a thousand years.*
5 *(The rest of the dead did not come to life until the thousand years were ended.) This is the first resurrection. Revelation 20:4-5 (NIV)*

God promised David a sure throne through his offspring. This covenant, however, would have one condition: disobedience in the Davidic family will be visited with chastisement, but the covenant of an aperture throne would stand as promised. The chastisement fell. The nation rebelled against God's laws. Israel stumbled into civil wars as Solomon's sons and generals fought for the throne which resulted in the nation being split; Rehobrom took the southern part, Judah; while Jeroboam took the northern part of Israel. Each claimed to be the king God had chosen.

Out of the twenty-two kings that served after Solomon's death, only eight were faithful to God's laws. This of course, caused the counties to suffer to the point that God even allowed the pagan empires of Assyria and Babylonia to destroy both kingdoms carrying them into exile. [1]

From that point of their history to now, the entire nation of Israel has never enjoyed the splendor and glory once known under the great kings David and Solomon. Instead, they suffered being painfully sandwiched between four rival world empires, each fighting for equal control over the Jewish people's lives. With little civil power allowed them, the opposing leaders tested it at a very costly price. That was not God's plan in the beginning. Instead, they were chosen to be a repository and channel through which the whole earth would one day be blessed. Though they failed in their part of the covenant, yet the agreement God made with David as found in **II Samuel 7:12-17** still stands.

If you would recall the question that the disciples ask Jesus, "Lord, will thou at this time restore again the kingdom back to Israel." This question striking indicates that they were well aware of Jesus royal descendant line to David, **Acts 1:6**. Naturally, Jesus chose not to deal with the question at the time. Nevertheless, it still bore proof that they clearly understood what David said in **Psalm 45:6:** Jesus Christ will resume power to the throne as a direct descendent.- according to **Acts 2:28,29**.

175

And, His throne will abide forever!

The Earth under new management
Isaiah 11:1-
*A shoot will come up from the **stump** of Jesse; from his **roots** as Branch will bear fruit. The Spirit of the Lord will rest on Him.*

*The Spirit of **wisdom and** understanding, the Spirit of **counsel** and of **power,** the Spirit of **knowledge** and of the fear of the Lord.*

*And, He will **delight** in the fear of the Lord. He will **not judge** by what he sees with His eyes, or decide by what he hears with His ears;*

*But, with righteousness He **will judge** the needy, with justice he will give decision for the poor of the earth. He will **strike the earth** with the rod of His mouth; with the breath of His lips He **will slay** the wicked.*

***Righteousness** will be his belt and faithfulness the sash around His waist.*

In the above passage there is a sort of world-view in which the Messiah as King appears. He will come forth from the house of Jesse, as a shoot-and revives the monarchy of the Davidic house. The shoot referred here implies that the royal house of David, once liken to a large oak tree had suffered being cut down. Yet, life remained in it, **Isaiah 6:13** and will once again bare fruit, as a new royal member will step forth to revive the monarchy.[2]

Jesus Christ as the **"new world leader"** will have super

176

natural qualities. That is: The Spirit of wisdom, discernment, the Spirit of counsel, and knowledge. He will judge the earth as no earthly King has ever done.

Hal Lindsey, in his book title *There is a New World Coming* states that Jesus reign on earth will usher in a **restored** nature, in both animal and vegetable life being at their highest state of development. Even desert plains will benefit and will portray a most beautiful idyllic picture of mountains covered with glorious pines, cedars, and redwood, reaching clear to the top of the highest peaks. [3]

The rays from the sun as it sweeps over the lovely landscape will help fill even the desert with flowers of every sort. Buttercups, daisies, poppies and marigolds, bluebells, and daffodils, hollyhocks and snapdogons, geraniums, and delphiniums, orchids and begonias, roses and, of course, the lilacs. Each with its own delicate design; its own special coloring and fragrance! [4]
The sun's warm rays will cause the flowers to turn eagerly toward the shining orb as ferns lift their fronds in joyous welcome. The desert plains and hillsides will be filled with masses of these flowers; all looking much like a multicolor carpet lay over the whole area. The fruit trees lay scattered looking like an art piece out of a picture book. *It will be an incredible view!*

While walking alone you will easily find small gold, silver, other precious stones lay glittering amid the lush grass and flowers.

And the wolf shall dwell with the lamb, and the leopard shall lie down with the kid, and the calf and the young lion and the fatted domestic animal together, and a little child shall be able to handle them. The cow and the bears shall feed side by side; their young shall lie down together; and the lion shall eat straw like the ox. A child will play by the cobra. These animals will not hurt or destroy My Holy Mountain. For the earth will be full of the knowledge of the Lord as the waters cover the sea
Isaiah 1 1:6-9 *author emphasis.*

Even the animal kingdom and reptiles will lose their ferocity and no longer be carnivorous. [5] So, don't be surprised to see a lamb jumping up and down on top of a lion playing with its tail! Leopards and cows shall gaze in the field together.

Christ's ruler ship shall be from sea even to sea, and from the river even to the ends of the earth. **Zechariah 9:10.** Antagonism between the northern and southern counties will forever cease, as the glory of the Lord will fill the entire earth!

A time of celebration!

Solomon said in the book of **Ecclesiastes 3:4**; a time to weep, and a time to laugh; a time to mourn, and a time to dance.

Rejoice over her, thou heaven, and ye holy apostles and prophets; for **God hath avenged** you on her.

AFTER these things I heard, as it were, a loud voice of a great multitude in heaven, saying, "Hallelujah! Salvation and glory and power belong to our God;

BECAUSE HIS JUDGMENTS ARE TRUE AND RIGHTEOUS; For he has judged the great harlot who was corrupting the earth with her immorality, and he **HAS AVENGED THE BLOOD OF HIS BOND-SERVANTS ON HER."**
And a second time they said, "Hallelujah! **HER SMOKE RISES UP FOREVER AND EVER."** and the twenty-four elders and the four living creatures fell down and worshiped God who sits on the throne saying, "Amen. Hallelujah!" **Revelation 18:20; 19:1-6.**

They shall be planted again

The "chosen people" of Israel and around the world have been dispersed to practically every part of the earth and have intermixed with numerous people. Starting with the era of the Canaanite, the Ammonites, the Horites, Hittites, and others. The Old Testament supports this statement; even during the Babylonian captivity, there was intermixture with many Mesopotamia people. [6]

And I scattered them among the heathen, and they were dispersed through the countries: according to their way and according to their doings I judged them. And when they entered unto the heathen, whither they went, they profaned my holy name, when they said to them, these are the people of the LORD, and are gone forth out of his land. **Ezekiel 36:19-20.**

The Jewish people will be restore back to their homeland: This is in line with the prophesy of Jeremiah.

179

Verse 37a Behold, I will gather them out of all countries, whither I have driven them in mine anger, and in my fury, and in great wrath; and I will bring them again unto this place,
Verse 38b; *and they shall be my people, and I will be their God:*
Verse 39; *And I will give them one heart, and one way, that they may fear me forever, for the good of them, and of their children after them.*
Jeremiah 32:37-39.

Over 400,000 have arrived in Israel since late 1989, boosting its population by nearly 10%. Israel took in 200,000 immigrants in 1990 and 170,500 in 1991, despite the disruptions caused by the Gulf War. Thousands are still continuing to come in spite of the temporary burden on the economy it creates. [7]

During the millennia, Israel will not be split again, but will be one nation with Jerusalem being the capital. They will be permanently established in the land **Ezekiah 34:28.** God will bring them into the land of Palestine, and they shall no longer be two nations-separate peoples, the one wanderer among the Gentiles, they shall be one nation upon the mountains of Israel.
Ezekiah 27: 21-22. According to Ezekiah they are permanently established in the land.

Verse 28; And they shall no more be prey to the heathen, neither shall the beast of the land devour them; but they shall dwell safely, and none shall make

them afraid. In addition, I will raise up for them a
plant of renown, and they shall be no more consumed
with hunger in the land, neither bears the shame of
the heathen any more. **Ezekiel 34:28-29**

The perpetual gates
All the land shall be turned into a plain from
Gaza to Rimmon, south of Jerusalem. Jerusalem
shall remain lifted up on its site and dwell in its
place, from Benjamin's gate to the place of the
former gate, to the Corner gate, and from
the Tower of Hanannel to the king's wine
presses. Moreover, it shall be inhabited, for there
shall be no more curse or ban of utter
destruction; but Jerusalem shall dwell securely.
Zechariah 14:12-11

You may recall in Chapter Eight my explanation of the
gates and walls natural purpose. Following that point,
a symbolical picture was given on those wall and gates
as well. Of course, the gates and walls played a vital
role, and stood as the important foundation of their
emotional, social, and economical lives from that point
of history to now. Apart from the costly mistakes Israel
made with their lives sometime, the scripture teaches
that *all believers* would suffer at the hand of satan;
including too, no one can be a true followers of Christ
without suffering attacks to their gates and wall as
mentioned above. Not every one suffered in the same
degree, but, as God's chosen people, all must be
prepared.

For even hereunto were you called: because Christ also **suffered for us,** leaving us an example, that you should **follow his steps.** 1 **Peter 2:21.**

Paul said that God would not put anymore on us than we could bear. **Hebrews 13:5.** Also, Christ, the Son of God, will perfect that which He has started in us unto that day of His return. **Philippians 1:6**

Jesus said: Rejoice you in that day, and leap for joy: for, behold, your reward is great in heaven: for in the like manner did their fathers unto the prophets. **Luke 6:38**

When Christ descends to Mount of Olives, **Zechariah 14:3,4** along with the rapture church He shall set up His kingdom on earth. Every gate or wall that satan destroys or damages Jesus shall restore it with His perpetual glory!
Yes, even from Benjamin's gate to the place of the former gate, to the Corner gate, and form the Tower of Hanannel to the king's wine presses-means the total aspect of the chosen people lives will be secure again. This time, forever!

A perpetual house
*And it shall come to pass in the last days, that the mountain of the **Lord's house** shall **be established** in the top of the mountains, and shall **be exalted** above the hills;*

and all nations shall **flow unto it**.

This *Solomon's Temple* was built in 922 B.C. in Jerusalem and in 950 B.C. dedicated as a centralized religious worship. This Temple stood as the historic symbol of Jewish religious glory and splendor. No temple before in history or since could compare with it in its magnificence. You can get a pictorial view of the **Dome on the Rock,** considered one of the wonders of the world from the southwest side of the city. Behind *The Dome* in the distance lies the Mount of Olives where Jesus will appear in glory! However, this beautiful Temple had undergone extensive repairs since being damaged due to ravages of the centuries, plus earthquakes now and then. [8]

It is the very site where the Prophet Daniel spoke of in **Chapters 9:27;** where the Anti-Christ will stand. Paul called him **the man of sin; ll Thessalonians 2:3,** will cause the oblation to cease and set up the abomination. He will then exalt himself above all that is called God, or that is worshipped; so that he as God sits in the temple of God, showing himself that he is God.
2 Thessalonians 2:4.

This superfluous and blasphemous act of the Anti-Christ will take place in the middle of the seven-year period of Israel's tribulation. He will seek to make the temple and other temple buildings desolate. This period will last about Three and one-half years. Nevertheless, when the King of Kings comes He will destroy the Anti-Christ and restore anew the Temple. This Temple shall out match the splendor of Solomon's Temple multitudinous times over. Many around the world will go to worship and see this glorious place in Jerusalem.

And many people shall go and say, Come ye, and let us go up to the mountain of the LORD, to the house of the God of Jacob; and he will teach us of his ways, and we will walk in His path; for of Zion shall go forth the law, and the word of the LORD from Jerusalem. **Isaiah 2:2,3.**

Israel is being restored to the place of God's favor as His peculiar and covenant people as promise according to (**Acts 3:21**). Hal Lindsey, a famous author who has written over eleven Christian books-including the best-selling Christian book in history, "The Late Great Planet Earth," says that Jerusalem will be the spiritual center of the entire world and that all people of the earth will annually worship Jesus who will rule there. (**Zechariah 14:16-22**).

The Jewish-believing remnant will be the spiritual leader of the world and will teach all nations the ways of the Lord. (**Zechariah 8:20-23**).[9]

I believe Hal Lindsey gave an accurate summary of (**Ezekiel 37**)that I believe best summed up the chosen people's *restoration.* I quote:
I encourage the reader to read (**Ezekiah 37 Chapters**) along with this insert from Hal Lindsey.

(Ezekiah 37:7-8) This phrase of scripture predicts the **PHYSCIAL RESTORATION** of the Nation without Spiritual life which began May 14, 1948.

Ezekiel 37:9-10; This phrase of the prophecy predicts the **SPIRITUAL REBIRTH** of the nation **AFTER** they are physical restored to the land as a nation. Hal goes on to say that **the graves** in Ezekiel symbolize the nation **being scattered. The coming together of the bones** and the **flesh** symbolizes the miracles of Israel's restoration to the land of Israel as a nation.

The fact that they have **no breath** is symbolic of having no spiritual life as yet. But the breath **from the Holy Spirit** will give life bring about the spiritual rebirth of the people.[10]

It's coming again!

In that day, says **Malachi 3:17,** the Lord shall gather His Jewels around the globe, and they shall be mine-says the Lord. Let the redeemed of the Lord say so. Weeping may endure for a night-(season), but **Joy will come** in the **morning. Psalms 30:5**

Dr. Martin Luther King, Jr., delivered one of the most powerful and monumental speeches, *"I have a dream,"* in August 28, 1963. A crowd of 200,000 witnessed a chilling speech that today still stands as relevant to the *restoration* respecting believers around the world. I grateful to how God Almighty use Dr. King in his life time, and with great pleasure I will *expand upon*

185

his words as the final word for restoration in this book.

I Have a Dream

"So I say to you, my friends, that although we must face the difficulties of today and tomorrow, it won't be long- America and the troubling world sweltering with the heat of injustice, oppression will be transformed one day into an oasis of freedom and justice. We will soon live in a nation and world where we will not be judged by the color of our skin or our religious background but by the content of our character.

Though prejudice still rings in the street of our cities and communities, yet, one day little Black, White, Mexican, Oriental, Jewish, and Asian boys and girls will join hands with each other as sisters and brothers. One day, we can walk the streets without fear of crime. No corruption in our government. Envy and strife will be no more for as we being the children of God we will work together, pray together, praise the Lord together. The wicked will cease from troubling and the weary will be at rest. Then all God's children-black men and white, Jew and Gentiles, Catholics and Protestants- will join hands and sing with joyfulness that old Negro spiritual song; an song which down through the centuries has declared that *Restoration* for our mean world is coming again soon. And when it comes we shall be- FREE AT LAST, FREE AT LAST, and THANK GOD ALMIGHTY **WE SHALL BE** FREE AT LAST! [11]

Bibliography

Books

Chapter One

Donald Peattie-, *"Natural History of Trees," published in 1978 (1) (2)*

The Oxford English Dictorary...1975..Publisher.... (3)

The Women's Book of World Records and Achievements (4)

Memorable Americans 1750-1950 (5)

Dean B. B Edwards's Encyclopedia (6)

Hank Hanegraaff -"*Counterfeit Revival*," (7)

The Hutchison Encyclopedia-Published by Helicon
http://www.helicon.co.uk (8)

Chapter Two

"Notre Dame Cathedral, Paris," *Temko, Allan-*
New York,Viking Press 1952
League of Women Voters of the United States/
"Woman Suffrage" Microsoft Encarta Encyclopedia
1999

Susan Banfield, -"The Fifteenth Amendment" (3)

"American Anti-slavery Society." Microsoft Encarta
Encyclopedia- 1999 (4) id

Bill J. Humble in the book entitled, " The American
Quest for the Primitive Church, 1988" (5)

E. Stanley Jones in his book entitled, "The
Reconstruction of the Church" 1970(6)

Richard T. Hughes in the book entitled, " The
American Quest for the Primitive Church- 1988(7)

Chapter Three
(1) Joe Esposito and Elena Oumano, "Good Rocking To Night"

Chapter Five:
(1) (2) (3) (4) New Analytical Bible: J.A. Dickerson Publishing Co. 1973

Chapter Six:
(1) (2)(3)New Analytical Bible: J.A. Dickerson Publishing Co. 1973

(4) Henry C. Link, Ph D. " The Return to Religion"-1937

(6) Uniform Crime Reports in 1992 and 1996.

(7) "Statistical Abstract of United States" 1996

(8) Dr. Silver-"American Psychiatric Associate."

(9) Suzanne Garment, in her 1991 book, *Scandal: "The Crisis of Mis-Trust in American Politics,

(11) Henry C. Link, Ph D. " The Return to Religion"-1937

Chapter Seven
(1) (2)The Pulpit Commentary by Joseph S. Exell, M.A; Hendrickson Publishers,

(2) Dale Carnegie- "How to stop worrying and start Living"- Definition of prayer with Dr. Alexis Carrel.

Chapter Eight
(1) "Handy Dictionary of the Bible by Merril C. Tenny-1965; Lamplighter Books

(2) Gerald Cowen-Sermon Starters from the Greek New Testament-1985

Chapter ELEVEN

(1) (2)(3)(4) "Christian Theology-Systematic and Biblical Studies"-Emery H. Bancroft.-1976

(5) "The Heart of Hebrew History"-H. I. Hester 1962

(6) "Encyclopedia Americana-Deluxe Library Edition"-Volume 15

(10) "Trumpet of Conscience- Martin Luther King. Jr.

Chapter TWELVE

(1) MacMillan-1987; Francis T.D. Jones-Bibliography on "Fountains"

(2) Webster's Third New International Dictionary

(3) MacMillan-1987; Francis T.D. Jones-Bibliography on "Fountains"

Chapter THIRTEEN

(1) There's A New World Coming" – Hal Lindsey

(2) There's A New World Coming" – Hal Lindsey

(3) There's A New World Coming" – Hal Lindsey

(4) 'The Bible Story"- Arthur S. Maxwell

(5) There's A New World Coming" – Hal Lindsey

(6) "The Abingdon Bible Commentary 1929

(7))"The Universal Jewish Encyclopedia-Volume

Two-1948
(8) "Temple Beyond Time" Arthur H. and Mina Klein.
(9) The Late Great Planet Earth"- Hal Lindsey
(10)"Road to Holocaust"- Hal Linsey
(11)There's A New World Coming" – Hal Lindsey
      " I Have A Dream"-Writings and Speeches that Changed the World- James Washington

Articles
(5) Anthony G. White, special report, entitled: "RESTITUTION AS A CRIMINAL SENTENCE
(9) Adult Video News", an industry trade publication
The Associate Press
(7) New York Time Articles 10/97
(8) New York Times Paper- Palestinians/Israeli Conflict 10/97
(9) New York Times Paper

Two books to be release

COMING SOON!!

"RESTORING THE BROKENSS WORKBOOK"
Exciting self-help Work booklet along with job descriptions

"THE SHATTERED VESSEL"
Why our lives becomes shattered and how it can be fix
again

Author, James M. Martin

FOR MORE INFORMATION CONTACT

J.M.MARTIN PUBLISHING
P.O.BOX 27364
LANSING,MI 48908
517-272-9481
E-Mail-Restor144.@AOL.com